The Teflon Self

How to Live Stress-Free in a Chaotic World

Edith del Mar Behr MD

www.delmimd.com

This book is dedicated to my sister and soul mate, Maria, whose ultimate promotion occurred on September 11, 2001.

She had the habit of referring to me as "God" and would lament how difficult it was to be the sister of someone so lofty. The reality is we just had a blast together, and in her space, nothing was impossible. I am in her space always now.

Sometimes she would say we were the same person just split in two when we were on our way into this world. I was the light side, and she was the dark side. Her side is equally beautiful and unparalleled, and now my light side is brighter and my dark side filled with incredible creativity.

Whenever you share a glass of Merlot with me, you will be in her presence. You will surely feel a rush, and there will be a moment when you laugh so hard there are tears in your eyes.

I love you, Maria.

Acknowledgments

I am so grateful to the love of my life, *Scot,* who fills my days with amazement, inspiration, and support. I met him after a funeral, and my great life has been magical ever since. I was blessed to have a passionately loving mom who thought I could do anything I put my mind to and a father who introduced me to the life of a seeker, though at the time I didn't get it. Now I do, I think.

My oldest, very Catholic son, *Max,* challenges me often and thinks I am crazy but loves me. He marches to his very unique drum and entertains me often.

My youngest son, *Hunter,* provides me with great hugs and happiness. He is one of the most self-assured and loving people I know.

My sons show me every day that even though their mother is independent and unconventional, she can still be well-adjusted and happy.

My best friends, *Susan, Kimmie,* and *Elysa,* support me in all I do and provide me with such great times too numerous to list, and if I told you about them, I might have to erase your memory!

Contents

Acknowledgments v

Introduction 1

Chapter 1. Choose Your Joy 9

Chapter 2. Listen to Your Inner Voice 49

Chapter 3. Take Back Your Power 59

Chapter 4. Live in Beauty and Gratitude 85

Chapter 5. Release Your Judgments 95

Chapter 6. Meditate and Breathe 115

Chapter 7. Imagine Your World into Reality 125

Conclusion 147

References 151

About the Author 157

Introduction

Let me start off by saying that I did not have a near death experience; no mystical experience either. I do not talk to the other side. I haven't had any life threatening cancers or health issues. I still eat fast food once in a while. I tried a macrobiotic diet once in my 20s, and it just made me feel weak. I probably don't have the discipline to do it right. I love a good dirty martini and honey berry flavored cigars. My only exercise lately is dancing in my kitchen and golfing. I admit I have exercised with a trainer in the past and actually enjoyed it sometimes; maybe I will do it again in the future.

Although I am a surgeon and that is not so common, I am faced with all the same life experiences most of us have. If I can become stress-free and tap into my inner spectacular self, you can connect to yours.

The Teflon Self lives life to the fullest and, even when "negative" experiences occur, handles them with ease. In fact, the negative experiences become less frequent and usually end up creating a benefit.

I am no different from anyone else, and yet, as we all are, I am unique, as there are no two of us that are exactly alike. I tried to fit in like we all do, and I guess I just wasn't strong enough to fit in. In my opinion, it really takes a huge amount of strength to "fit in" and not end up dead or addicted to heroin. So obviously I wanted to find another way because I didn't want to do heroin or die.

Honestly, I tried to do it my way when I was young and got burned, not badly, but I am a pretty sensitive person or at least not willing to hurt.

So like many of us who get burned or have children or both, we conform. Though we are willing to risk our lives doing what we think is "wrong" or "dangerous" or "not respectable" before children, once we have children we usually act "responsibly." If we experience a negative consequence because we pushed the limits of ourselves or the rules, we also then decide to conform.

Maybe someday I will write the "tell all" story, but for now let's just say that I experimented like many of us do in our youth to various degrees. I experienced minor consequences because of my guilt. I think that all consequences are because we believe we will have them, and our feeling guilty brings them on…but that is for another book.

One of those consequences was my first son, and so because of the consequence and now being responsible for this beautiful little baby, I conformed.

I got life insurance and got married to a man I didn't love, thinking I could make any sacrifice to keep this small being from experiencing any hardship. But I digress; the tell-all book will have to wait. Suffice it to say I found myself living a normal life and feeling miserable eight years later.

Now I know many of you have conformed to a life of quiet desperation for much longer, probably because you didn't recognize it as such. You swallowed the belief that life is a struggle with a few good moments in between. Perhaps you are a freer spirit and ended up addicted to heroin or somewhere in between.

Whichever path you found yourself following, for no one would consciously choose the life of quiet desperation or addiction on purpose, *now you are open to another way.*

There are those who live lives that fit in well with society, who were meant to be there. I have a good friend who has a very normal life and is one of the happiest people in the universe. In fact, she is one of the people I admire the most in this world. It is not because she follows the norm but because she is true to herself and is happy about everybody else who finds happiness in whatever way they find it. She has been a constant source of support and unconditional love for my nonconforming life.

In 1996 I could not stand my life. On the surface, it looked like everything was wonderful. I was a general surgeon, I was the senior partner in my practice, I had a successful husband, and he seemed to adore me. We had children, and they were very cute and healthy. I was considered good looking and talented in many ways. My list of blessings was endless. It seemed like I had it all together. I had everything anyone could want. That was the surface picture.

In reality, I was completely stressed out at work. I could never get ahead of my paperwork or my schedule. I rushed through encounters with my patients, never really getting to sit down and talk with them. I was just removing diseased organs and fixing things without healing the person. That was NOT the way I wanted to practice medicine.

Meanwhile, on the home front, my stepchildren and I were at war. I had never experienced such anger and hostility, and the tension was affecting my relationship with my own son. My husband was very critical and angry with me every day for things such as coming home late from work. I wasn't exactly open to his comments. "Excuse me? I'm a surgeon!"

I was independent and wanted to do things my way, but I found myself living in HIS house—a house which had been decorated by his previous wife, not me. We did things his way because I didn't want to deal with his anger, and on some level, I was trying to get his approval.

I was also unhappy with my body. I was starting to see signs of aging and couldn't seem to find time to work out or even get a facial. I was also out of touch with my friends because I was so "busy."

I felt like I was on a treadmill and under stress at every moment. Even vacations were stressful. I would worry about what I didn't do before I left and what I would have to do once I got back. Then I would even worry about not having accomplished enough fun activities while on vacation!

Nothing in my life was in any way truly difficult, and yes I did find many moments of enjoyment, but even they were clouded by what I didn't do or still needed to do or obligations looming in the horizon.

I would expect to have time to work on some of my other skills, and that never seemed to happen either. The worst thing was that I had reached all the accepted goals for success, and I still wasn't truly happy or fulfilled. The next big change I could expect would be retirement, some 20 plus years in the future. I realized that I had nothing to look forward to for the next 20 years! This was it. There was no school to finish, no practice to establish, no knight in shining armor on the horizon.

I felt sorry for myself and burnt out. My life felt joyless and full of struggle. I felt guilty for any fragment of joy I did experience because I had not accomplished enough with all the talents God had given me. I constantly reprimanded myself for not doing enough and felt sorry for myself because I wasn't happy.

Even if I got a massage or facial, on that rare occasion I hid this from my family and my office because I felt guilty for indulging myself. I didn't lie about it. I just didn't mention it to anyone. Like a lot of things in my life.

If you asked anyone about me, other than my husband at the time, they would have told you I was a confident, fun-loving, free spirit. To many others, I looked like I had the perfect life. To me, it was anything BUT perfect!

I had reached a point in my life with no goals and nothing that would give me hope for a happy future. It was like being a rabbit chasing a carrot and finally realizing how mindless and futile that is.

On August 15, 1996, I declared, *"There has to be another way to live! Even though I don't know how to do it yet, I want to feel joyful and happy and innocent and full of excitement about the future."*

I was open to help, and the universe stepped into that opening. You can call it God, Spirit, Source, Divine Intelligence, or any other name you want—a rose is still a rose no matter what you call it.

I remembered how wonderful life felt when I was five, innocent and guilt-free. I put out an SOS to God, a cry out to the universe for help. I wanted to know how to live with joy and love. I wanted to know what the other way was. I "had it all," but I was willing to give it all up because none of it felt right. I needed a radical change, and I wanted to avoid learning the hard way by getting cancer or losing my job or going through any other trauma that might finally wake me up.

I read the *Celestine Prophecy* by James Redfield because two people recommended it to me in one month. This was my path into the world of self-help books and tapes. I discovered Deepak Chopra, Wayne Dwyer, Jane Roberts, and Neale Donald Walsh. Their writing echoed how I felt and what I wanted for my own life.

From these books and many others and even more CDs and cassette tapes (if you remember them), I distilled four major concepts that would later help me turn my life around:

1. All that happens is exactly as it should be. There are no mistakes.

2. All personal interactions are an exchange of energy— either giving it or trying to get it. I am completely responsible for these interactions, and there are no exceptions.

3. There is an infinite source of energy called *Love*. It is available to anyone directly from the source in infinite supply. When you try to get it through others without the source, you fail every time.

4. I am one with all that is, and the world I live in is a direct reflection of what is inside of me.

I applied them without exception to every circumstance. I decided not to "cut anything out" of my life or change anything externally until I figured "it" out; "it" being what life was all about.

It was a fairly large endeavor now that I think about it, but that was my request. Within a few months, I was free of all struggle and stress. People actually came up to me and asked what had happened because I was so happy and at peace.

This book, *The Teflon Self*, is a summary of what works for me. Sit back and enjoy reading it, for if you don't enjoy reading it, then it isn't the book for you. You will discover some new concepts and ideas about life and how to practically apply them.

CHAPTER 1

Choose Your Joy

If you're reading this, you're probably searching because something in your life is not going the way you want it to go. Am I right? You want to find out how to make your life fit your idea of what you want it to be. You may want to fix a specific part of it, or you may not exactly know what is wrong, but you know something isn't right. Possibly, you aren't sure that what you would like is feasible.

Everything you really want in life boils down to wanting some form of love: approval, acceptance, prestige, pleasure, a sense of security. Everyone is searching for the feeling of love, but we have confused the car or money or job or relationship or _____ (you fill in the blank), anything that seems like a path to this feeling, with the actual experience of love.

But it's not really any of those things or experiences that you want. It's the feeling of love that you want. And you can have that feeling anytime you want by *choosing* to have it. The irony is that once you choose to have the feeling of love, all of the things and experiences that you want show up. One of the secrets of successful living is to:

> Allow yourself to have the feelings you want independent of the circumstances that surround you.

When you learn to evoke the feelings you want regardless of what is going on around you, the circumstances that surround you will change to reflect your feelings.

You don't have to earn the feelings. Just bring it on. Then, the activities you choose will be what you want, and you will be passionate about them. You will be able to love passionately and with abandon, no holds barred. That love will be returned to you in even greater amounts without all the anxiety and doubt and heartache.

How to Evoke a Feeling

Imagine that you are looking at your sleeping child or pet. This precious being looks so beautiful to you. He or she doesn't have to do anything to earn your love. You remember how that feels and how beautiful those moments are. Recreate that feeling by imagining those scenes in your mind. Now, *send that same feeling to yourself.*

The other way to recreate the feeling of love is to remember and recreate a scenario where you were so filled with gratitude and love for another or yourself. You have the ability to recreate that scene and feeling, or if there is no memory to recreate, you can imagine one into existence.

Just take time out to think about one item in your life that you are thankful for and realize how many people were involved in getting that item to you. It may be a glass of water.

You can thank the earth for providing the water and material for the glass. You can thank the factory that made the glass and all the workers involved. You can thank the factory owners for developing the means to provide that glass. You can thank the delivery company and vehicle driver. You can thank the store that sold it. You can thank the water plant for purifying the water and so on. When you get going, you start to feel so grateful to so many people that gave you the pleasure of a glass of water. This could get more detailed and elaborate, but you get the point.

Give yourself permission to imagine, pretend, and create the feeling, whatever feeling you want. The more you do this, the more real it becomes, and in less time than you think, what you imagine becomes "real life." You can practice imagining what you want into reality anytime, anywhere, without taking time out of your day, telling anyone else about it, or writing anything down. You can give yourself permission to have that feeling any time you choose.

Let's look at a few applications of this principle. Here's how my friend applied the principle of evoking a feeling to change her circumstances.

My Friend's Car

One of my girlfriends wanted a sports car. At the time, she was driving a typical "mom" car and feeling resentment toward her husband and *his* sports car. I told her to pretend she had the car she wanted and to play with the feelings she got, to pretend she was getting looks from other people as she drove by, etc. She actually had so much fun with this that it became part of her driving experience. She no longer felt resentful and found more joy in the moment.

In less than a year, she had a sports car. The novelty wore off after a couple of months, but she continued to find more and more joy using the creative process she had learned. Now she can be and do anything, freeing her to go after what she truly wants rather than chasing after desires born of advertisements and misconceptions.

She ultimately realized that she wanted a luxury sedan, not really a sports car, and this is her reality now. The knowledge imagination is even more exciting to her than that car, I might add.

Another Example

When I divorced my second husband (another story for the "tell-all" book), I was looking for a house to move into. I used the same technique I taught to my friends. I didn't really work at finding what I wanted, but I knew what it would feel like. I pretended that feeling as often as I could. Someone suggested I take a look at a development that was close to where I worked, and though I was resistant to the idea of a development, I checked it out anyway.

When I walked through the model home, it felt exactly like what I imagined, and I ended up buying that home and moving in a few months later. It still feels amazing to be here, and when I moved in, I was easily able to have it furnished and ready the next day. It was seamless and easy, and everything from settlement to the move went smoothly.

I have been divorced twice, and though my first divorce was traumatic in so many ways, my second divorce was easy and amicable and went exactly the way I wanted it to. Everyone was okay with it and in some ways relieved. I am still on friendly terms with my ex-husband, his new wife, and my step children.

That was another event in my life that I imagined into reality. Imagining how events will go is like pretending to have conversations with the people involved and having them convey to you that they are okay with whatever it is you are doing. You send them love, and they send it back to you.

Loving Your Body

Do you like the way you look? I tell myself I am gorgeous every day. When you decide to see yourself this way, others will too, guaranteed!

Forget about changing your body at first and concentrate on changing your mind. Your physical reality will follow.

Perhaps you think that if you were thinner, you would be more lovable and feel better about yourself. These are just arbitrary limitations you put on yourself. You tell yourself you can't accept love until you are in those states of physical appearance.

The truth is that even skinny and pretty people often feel unloved. It's all arbitrary and relative anyway. You may be attractive to one person and not to another. You may seem thin to someone, heavy to another, and too thin to the next.

The most attractive quality you can have is to know how wonderful you are. Those people who have that kind of magnetism are usually not the most physically attractive among us, but they exude self-confidence and the knowledge that they are a gift to whomever they are near. They are not in any way looking for your acceptance; they have already gotten it from themselves.

It is ironic how many people get a new body or look from plastic surgery or working out and still don't seem to be happy. If you work on your inner self, you will have something that will serve you until the day you move on to the next life. It has nothing to do with being a "good person," so don't confuse the two. There are many who do "good" acts that are not attractive. On the other hand, those that are truly attractive usually are involved in good acts, but you will not know about it. They are living their truth in all things.

If you don't like your self-image, stop looking in mirrors. Or if you do, pay attention to aspects of yourself that you like. Enhance them, and don't be afraid to flaunt your beautiful hair or eyes or hands. If you desire any changes, imagine them into your reality and act the part. As you act the part, you will be surprised by how much it will become who you are.

Focus on what you want to be and avoid the pitfall of making comparisons, even in your mind. Celebrate others' success as if it were your own. When someone makes strides in any area, pretend that it is you or that you have had a similar success. Because we are all connected, it is actually true in a sense.

Avoid "beauty" magazines—they're designed to make you feel inadequate and jealous. If you have the resources, get a professional photographer and make-up artist to photograph you, and you will understand how truly gorgeous you can be given that advantage. You will never feel inadequate when looking at a fashion magazine again.

Get clear about how you want your body to look and feel. If you are looking for approval from others, no matter what you do to your body, there will always be someone who doesn't approve. Why wait for approval? Give it to yourself now.

Love you, dream you, imagine you, enjoy you, and miracles will happen. So many times we plan to make an improvement and it doesn't happen for many reasons. Even when it does, we seem to slowly end up back where we started. There is a simple reason for this, and it is because you haven't loved, dreamed about, imagined, and enjoyed yourself into the state of being that supports the new you.

Relationships

How would your life be different if you thought everyone already loved you deeply? Well, they do. Don't let their ignorance to that fact stop you from enjoying your glorious life.

> Assume that everyone is madly in love with you!

No matter what they do, just interpret their actions as if they were head over heels about you. If they are not nice or even downright rude, assume they just don't know how to show their true feelings or can't admit it to themselves.

When you do this, the actions of other people take on a whole new meaning, and you walk through life with a different feeling. In truth, all people are in love with all people. They may have forgotten that truth, but now that you know it, you can live it and ignore the actions of those who have forgotten.

It is an interesting phenomenon but one I live with every day and that is when you know something it becomes your reality. When you know that everyone loves you, you are then surrounded by those that love you.

Loneliness

So many people feel lonely. Yet we are in a world *filled with people!* There are so many to love and so many who want to love. One of my patients told me that she was doomed to loneliness because all of her family was gone or lived far away. Who made the rule that love is only reserved for blood relatives?

There are lots of ways to be with people if you truly allow it. If you are lonely, look at why you are not reaching out to other people. The reason is always fear. Isn't it ironic that we fear the thing we want most?

Don't be afraid of reaching out to people in friendship or romance or partnership. The worst thing that can happen is that it doesn't work out. If you never reach out, you will never know. It might be that the worst mistake you make can be a lead to your most treasured relationship. If you don't take any steps, you can't go anywhere. The beauty is that we are in a sea of people at all times. You have to work at being lonely. Stop working at that and allow yourself to be connected.

When I say work, I don't mean work but rather play with the idea of being involved. If you have a lot of subconscious baggage in that area, then try imagining the way you want it to be. Imaginary friends or an imaginary partner can be the first step to really living what you want.

You will find that many times, even though you say you want to have friends or a partner, you believe relationships come with obligations and compromise. Freedom could be lost, and we are all freedom-based beings. Seriously, the relationships that you form when you get your source of love supplied infinitely will be without obligations and compromise and increase your freedom.

Work on getting in tune with your source, and you won't have any loneliness in your life ever.

Attraction and Romance

Maybe you want a loving relationship. I constantly hear from people that they can't seem to find a Mr. or Ms. "Right." This is a prime area to practice the following principle of attraction: Give yourself permission to feel loved from the inside, and you will create love all around you, drawing others to you who love themselves and are capable of loving you.

Maybe you're in a relationship, but it doesn't feel loving. Assume that those you are in relationship with feel the way you want them to feel about you. Any actions that are in conflict with what you want you can attribute to the other person's inner pain or insecurity. It's not about you! It becomes clear that you don't have to control another person to find your own self-love.

It's hard to believe, but the only reason we don't have the love we want is because we are telling the universe constantly that we don't want it—we aren't ready or worthy, or we are too afraid to change anything. When you get clear about your total responsibility in this arena, you begin to see how easy it is to change the circumstances of your love life. Ask yourself, "Why have I chosen this?" It is more difficult than you think to accept a loving, wonderful partner in life without loving yourself first. Actually, it is impossible.

If you want to be funny or sexy or lovable, tell yourself you are. You are always surrounded by people who reflect how you think of yourself no matter how much you protest. Change how you think of yourself, and you will see the magic happen in the people around you.

I would recommend having your imaginary lover or friend tell you all the things you want to hear often during the day and visualize that you have already done romantic dinners and trips and whatever it is you think would be part of your ideal relationship.

> Pretend God is madly in love with you, and imagine what He or She would say to you.

Each time you see a beautiful sky or landscape or flower, assume it is a gift of love from the divine, your first true love.

Practice this, and you will have little time in your life for worry, guilt, or negativity. Life will become fun and alive and passionate.

Here's another secret for living a stress-free, happy life:

> If you are happy and feeling joy, move toward that, and if you are not, move away.

Life is very simple; all you have to do is go toward fun and happiness and move away from struggle and sadness. This idea makes some people feel uncomfortable. It may sound diametrically opposed to everything you ever heard in your church, synagogue, mosque, or school. I'll say it again: Do what you like to do and stop doing what you don't like to do. Life is short. Why waste it on what you don't like?

Most people don't follow this basic principle and misinterpret their feelings or lie to themselves in order to keep the status quo. Why? Because they are afraid of losing whatever love (or substitutes for love) they have found. It's worth confronting this fear and making a choice—when you decide to move towards joy, your life becomes fluid and effortless. You can be the work of art you were meant to be without breaking a sweat.

The following is an example of my life *before* I learned to move toward joy. I used to unconsciously choose partners that I felt superior to in some way so that I could see myself as a blessing to them and, of course, be in control in a subtle way. The result was disillusionment and boredom and no passion or deep connection to draw upon when the waters got choppy. I was afraid of rejection and deep emotion. If they didn't live up to my expectations, I could easily blame them and leave.

I found reasons to avoid people who attracted me before I could even be conscious of possible rejection. The more I was attracted to someone, the more reasons and excuses I made to avoid even trying.

I jumped into being attracted to people who were emotionally or physically unavailable as my next self-protection angle. When previous relationships don't work, many of us make sure we don't get into another one by always seeming to want what we can't have.

We seem to think that it is the circumstances out there that control us, but it is always a conscious or subconscious choice that we make. It became clear that I wanted something different, and I was ready for it. I addressed my issues with relationships, and everything I wanted manifested.

Now that I have learned to move TOWARDS joy, the world of my relationships is completely different. I can no longer be rejected because I love myself unconditionally. When I love someone, it doesn't matter what their response is. If they spend time with me, however long or short it is, it is a gift. I enjoy the person passionately without concern for tomorrow.

The difference this has made is that I have great passion in my life in all my relationships and a partner who is my equal—exciting, passionate, available, romantic—someone who I would have been so afraid of in the past.

Here's another secret to success, one I learned the hard way after I found myself working harder and harder and having less and less pleasure:

> Success is not born of hard work. Success is born of doing what you love.

When you're doing what you love, you may appear to be working hard, but in reality you are having a blast. If you are waiting for your success to happen because of all your hard work, you will be sadly disappointed. So many people give themselves ulcers and heart attacks trying to reach a level of success by working at something they don't truly enjoy, let alone feel passionate about doing. If you look around, there is no rhyme or reason to how the world rewards hard work.

If you are "stuck" in a job or business that you don't enjoy, the easiest way to get "unstuck" is to find what you do like about it and focus on that. Find a way to enjoy the people you work with, which will become so much easier as you love yourself unconditionally and look for the good in the situation. Then visualize how you want your life to be as often as you can daily.

I know it is difficult to avoid some activities you don't like in our world, such as paying taxes or getting up in the morning with your alarm clock, but as you find the aspects of those activities that are good—and there is always good to find or imagine—you will find that solutions magically happen that make those activities become less of a drain.

My dad once said to me when I complained about paying taxes that I should be thankful I make enough that I can pay that much in taxes. Bless any outflow of money you have so that you can receive even more.

On the other hand, there are many aspects of life that we feel are absolutely necessary that aren't. Get very selfish about what you engage in. If something is not fun and not absolutely necessary and the only consequence is disapproval from someone, cut it out of your life or moment. Realize that disapproval from others is their way of controlling you. Your effort to get or keep their approval is your attempt to control them. Once you get that and work on unconditionally loving yourself and ridding yourself of guilt, you will find no disapproval enters your world.

Operating Room Lessons

There is a lot of external pressure on surgeons to RUSH. I used to try to go fast because I was taught that, to be successful, I had to be quick and efficient, not only in the operating room but in interacting with patients as well. This was draining all the pleasure out of my practice, and I was always running behind. I wanted to get to know each patient and connect, not see someone as just a diseased gallbladder.

21

I decided that I would allow my joy and pleasure and take my time. Each patient received as much time as he or she needed to chit chat, answer questions, address fears, uncover the psychological aspects of the illnesses, and do as much education as was needed or wanted. The miracle was that I began to get more done in less time! I now get out of work on time, and I don't keep my patients waiting because I am running behind (sometimes they used to have to wait for an hour or more!). I am still amazed at this every day.

Once I stopped pushing and just let go of the need to control my schedule, I found that my schedule flowed with perfect timing. Even better was my enjoyment of the experience and each patient. I don't feel like I work at all but just enjoy each new experience and the relationships that result.

In the operating room, I work "in the zone" with ease and confidence. I know there is a greater power working through me, and I trust and enjoy it more and more. I feel at ease, and I am detached from the outcome of the surgery. I know that I am doing my best in each moment, and the rest is out of my hands.

In other words, I don't ever feel guilty, worried, or anxious about my performance. I find that my patients do very well and heal on many levels, not just their physical problems. My work is a joy and a constant source of miracles. I keep focused on the gift I am given to be able to act as the healer in these circumstances. It makes all of it so sacred and beautiful. How can that be work?

Money

I used to have many conflicting beliefs about money and hard work. I made a comfortable living, but I still felt that I was always struggling to make ends meet. I worked long hours and felt that I wasn't doing enough. This feeling of inadequacy surfaced whenever I saw or heard of someone who worked more hours or who had accomplished more in his/her life, made more money, etc. I also felt that I could not justify my salary based on how hard I worked. The guilt surrounding my ability to make more money surfaced whenever I saw someone who had less than I did.

Everyone wants more money, but we often judge others that have more to be unhappy, to have "given something up" for it, or to be morally corrupt or stingy. If we think having more is bad for us, then why would we want more? How hard must one work for money? How many hours a week warrants how much? What amount of education and training is required for what salary? None of this makes sense.

The evidence of what actually happens in life supports that there is no rhyme or reason to why some make a lot of money and others don't. The only thing that makes any sense is that you experience what you believe you will experience.

I also thought that if I received what I wanted, someone else had to lose something. I finally realized that I deserve as much money as I want to have. I can have it without negative side effects, and so can everyone else. I realized that my having more does not take away from anyone else having more.

Changing Beliefs about Money and Work

I want to tell you how I shifted my own beliefs about money and work. First, I established clearly in my mind that we are all equal. No human is worth more or less than another. How much a person has materially is often not related directly to anything about him or her. Rewards are not necessarily proportional to how much someone works or how hard, nor to character, contribution to society, intelligence, or talent.

Whether you spend your life raising children or saving the world, whether you have three degrees after your name or none, whether you work hard or have everything handed to you on a silver platter, no one is inherently better than anyone else. The bum on the street could be a master in disguise here to teach a grand lesson. We have no way of knowing the truth of anyone's path. The fact that a being exists makes him or her worthy of all the world has to offer.

If you believe you deserve money or if a group of people believe you deserve it, then you get it. Why depend on a group of people? Just believe it yourself. When I realized this, my feelings of inadequacy and guilt subsided. I did not have to do a thing to be equal to anyone! Everyone who didn't have what I had was now responsible for his or her situation completely. I now know that.

In addition, I also realized that the more I attracted into my own life the more I could bless others. In fact, I am starting to believe that the more successful I become the more successful others become.

> Every person has the choice to be where he or she wants to be and has the capacity to choose something different to change the situation.

I decided to choose differently and from that moment on, I felt good about myself. I also felt close to people that I had previously found annoying or judgmental because they no longer annoyed me or judged me. It is a universal phenomenon that you are only judged when you judge, and you are only annoyed when you annoy. The world is truly a reflection of the inner you. Change that and watch the world change before your eyes.

Now I never work. I just play every day at my job. My hours are reasonable, and I am not struggling to make ends meet. At the same time, I have manifested more enjoyable activities and material things in my life. Again, I am in awe of the constant joy in my life, no matter what happens. I am no longer plagued by feeling guilty, inadequate, angry, frustrated, impatient, or stressed. Instead, I feel great about myself and everyone else in my life.

I have found that the quickest way to attain a stress-free, happy life is to first clarify your goals and then *decide* that your path will flow easily. (It doesn't *have* to flow easily and happen quickly. You can make it hard and slow if you want. That's up to you.) When I say clarify your goals, I mean to get clear about what it is that you want. All of the goals you set and things you want and desire for achievements are about joy and happiness— either yours or that of someone you love.

The best way to do any of this is to let go of your attachment to any structure or plan you have to achieve your many goals. That doesn't mean not to have plans and structure, just don't get attached. Keep looking at your goals and making sure they ring true to your desires and are not placed there by outside sources. These sources may be other people, institutions, communities, parents, or religions. These sources can be helpful in certain circumstances, especially when you don't know your path, but don't become dependent on them.

What you think you deserve and believe within yourself is what will happen.

We are taught that the road of life has to be difficult; you have to struggle to get anything worthwhile. We believe you have to endure hardships and sacrifices and suffering. If you find joy in that, great, go with that. But if that is not what you want, you don't have to continue to live that way. In fact, I would venture to say that hardship and struggle only keep you from your goals and what will truly make you happy.

It's Not about Working Harder

I have no desire to work hard or struggle. I want to enjoy my life in a big way. If you feel more important because you worked hard to "get where you are," then you are putting out to the universe that working hard to get places is what you want. More of the same will then come your way. If that is what you want, then you go for it. However, you can choose to do it the easy way like I do.

Choosing the Easy Way

Of course, choosing this way means you have to be comfortable with everyone else finding life easy too. Can you handle that? Now, how will you determine your worth? You won't have anyone to feel better than or have anyone to look up to you and admire your hard work and diligence. This means giving up that specific idea about yourself. It means letting go of judgment about what is right, wrong, better, or worse because none of it really is. Get very clear about what you want and whether you are conveying that desire or its opposite.

Remember, one of the secrets of successful living is to allow yourself the feelings you want independent of the circumstances that surround you. When you do that, the circumstances that surround you adjust to mirror what you feel and think. Your thoughts and the way you use them create your feelings. Some of your early programming is so ingrained that the thoughts are instantaneous and compressed, not even in word form but rather as an unconscious force that affects you before you can negate it. It's important to learn how to bring your thoughts out in the open where you can remove and replace worn out ideas and beliefs that are affecting your life.

When people comment that I must have worked hard to become a physician, I always reply that I truly did not experience the process that way; I saw many others working much harder. I enjoyed my educational years and did not drive myself to be a surgeon. It just happened.

Perhaps when you are on the right path, the universe won't let you fail no matter how hard you try to screw it up. In my early years, I often put short-term pleasure before studying, filling out paperwork, or getting loans. My education was slowed down while I was in a custody battle for my son. And yet I kept being guided back to the surgical path. It was just something I loved. It seemed like the force of God kept putting me where I could do my work, and I just seemed to always fall into where I was supposed to be.

The Easy Way Out

I do not like hardship, pain, or struggle, and I found myself naturally drawn to the "easy way out," as they say. I felt guilty about this because I didn't think this was the "right" way. I always thought I should have tried harder, worked harder, but in the end I always gravitated to what thrilled me.

I was born intense and enthusiastic but not too attached to a particular path, and when the going got tough, I just found another way to go. Of course, when you are thrilled or passionate about something or someone, nothing seems difficult. I was just going toward the maximum pleasure area, even though, at the time, I often felt guilty about that. Now I don't bother with the guilt because I have found over and over again that this direction works.

Releasing Fear

As we get older, our fears, experiences, and pressures from society often make us play it safe. We lose touch with who we were meant to be and become robots doing what everyone else is doing. No wonder life doesn't seem as intense as when we were teenagers nor as carefree as when we were children. We buy into the fallacy that this is the way it is supposed to be. No, no, no! It is not the way it is supposed to be.

The problem is that, when we get burned, there are few alive enough to help us find the true lesson in the burn. What we get mostly is someone telling us to play it safe like they do. When I looked clearly at those playing it safe and realized that I couldn't live my life that way, I was forced to look at my "mistakes" again through a different lens. The times we are burned are the times we walk into a fire without preparation. Let me prepare you for any fire.

> Your life is supposed to be everything your heart desires it to be.

You were born with the ability to live this way no matter how far off the track you have gotten or how old you are! Creating the life we were meant to have is easy if and when we release our fears. Let's look at a few common fears that hold us back.

Fear of Loss

Stress is all about fear, usually fear of losing something. It could be the fear of losing approval or life or love or money. If you are stressed because of your job, it is because you are afraid of rejection or losing your job. Perhaps you are afraid of looking for another job. It always comes down to some kind of fear. To release your fears, you have to love yourself unconditionally no matter what you are experiencing.

There are other fears that we are programmed to have throughout life, such as fear of the unknown, of death, of loss of a loved one, or loss of anything for that matter. If you are motivated to address all of your fears squarely, you will see that every person experiences all of these things and lives through them. You will see that you can handle anything, and the fear will go away. You no longer give it power over you. This doesn't mean that you want undesirable things to happen, but you know that there is a purpose to all things, and you refrain from giving energy to these fears.

Facing your fears head on is like turning on the light in a dark room and recognizing there is nothing to fear. Of course, you have to own your eternal self and divine ability to create your own reality to truly turn the light on, but still most of our fears are based on outdated ideas and beliefs that we consciously don't recognize.

For example, being afraid of confrontation with a coworker who actually has no power over you may be related to having your parents yell at you. Now anyone who is loud makes you want to cringe, and you avoid confrontation. That kind of issue is usually cured by bringing it out in the open and looking at it and seeing how silly it really is at this point in your adult life.

Life is short for all of us in this physical world—you can't change that, so why not enjoy every moment that you have instead of wasting it on worrying. If you believed that you were eternal and unlimited and had all the time you wanted, you still wouldn't worry because what would be the point. Really, in all circumstances, fear serves no purpose.

Knowing to avoid a dangerous activity is different from fear, and having a heightened awareness when involved in activities that could end this particular journey in your eternal existence is also another thing. I just wanted to be clear that there are times in life when fear and caution are appropriate, but for the most part, our lives are not like that. In fact, if they are, we are choosing that on some level or actively choosing it consciously.

Creating the life we want requires us to learn how to have intense feelings about something without being attached to results or outcomes. This is one of the ways to create events, relationships, and stuff in this physical world. It's important to regain our ability to have intense feelings and to let go of all the baggage we have taken on through our lives. Ironically, detaching actually allows you to be more intense and passionate.

> However you imagine the process, easy or hard, is how it will be.

For myself, I chose an easy journey. I want to go up the slope of the mountain that is clearly marked with plenty of fun along the way. Tomorrow I may choose a more challenging route and change my mind. Who knows?

To get rid of your fear, you must learn to love unconditionally. And in order to love unconditionally, you will have to connect to your own divinity and the divinity of others. Begin to experience yourself as more than your physical presence and realize that there is more to this human experience than we can explain with our limited perception, understanding, and knowledge.

Fear of Death

The fear of death, our own or that of a loved one, is the key fear we have to face if we are to live without stress and find joy in every moment. When I took some time out to work on this fear, I realized that this life is a brief experience compared to eternity. Everyone in my life is playing a part. As beings, they are not limited to the roles of "mother," "sister," or "child." I came to know that love is forever and essence is forever. Once we are connected, we are always connected. I know when someone leaves this world it is of their choosing, no matter the circumstances. Even if you lived to be a thousand, you would want more time and probably grieve over the youngster who died at 500. It is all arbitrary.

September 11th and My Sister

On September 11, 2001, in the North Tower of the World Trade Center, my sister (soul mate, best buddy, and person

I wanted to retire with) made the transition to her next life. Though I may cry with deep emotion on occasion, it is with gratitude for the gift of her life, then and now. I do not question the events. I know they had to be. I felt, and still feel, her presence around me and through all of my loved ones. I know I will see her again. She was and is someone whom I deeply love, and I know she has entered a glorious state of being.

I have not felt a nanosecond of anger or hatred toward anyone, only deep inspiration at the outpouring of love that I saw. I have continued to feel joy and happiness, and I have not changed how I live because of this event because I was already living my truth. I am thankful for having released my fear of death prior to her "promotion" and thankful that I had my priorities straight—spending time with the people I love while I can so I have no regrets.

You can experience tragedy and loss without stress and depression. You can honor the love you have with that person in continuing your joyful life with wonderful memories and new, expanded relationships.

Fear of Change

It's ironic that we are all so afraid of change when change is the only thing we can count on in life. The only thing that doesn't change is the real inner you and the sharing of love.

You may have buried this part of yourself, sometimes called the inner child. It's the part of you that comes out to gaze in wonder at the sunset over the ocean, the part of you that looks in awe at the one you love, that connects with the hug of a child, that questions the unquestionable. You may have locked it up in your subconscious mind, but it's the part of you that has never forgotten that life is supposed to be about love. It is the part of you that came here to experience joy and newness and growth and freedom and creativity.

Love is sharing the energy that is YOU with another person or the whole world. The problem is that we are so out of touch with who we are that it is difficult to share that energy for a prolonged period of time. Yet that is exactly what every one of us wants to do at every moment we exist.

Being in Love All the Time

Imagine how you felt when you were madly in love, however briefly. I bet you would give anything to be able to feel that way all the time. Remember how so many things didn't matter, like having money or a nice car? You probably felt attractive to the one who loved you, and it didn't matter what anyone else thought. You weren't noticing. The quirks or flaws of the person you were in love with just made them more attractive. If they had an old broken down car, you became fondly attached to old broken down cars.

Now if you see an old broken down car, you probably make judgments about the kind of person driving it. You are probably seeking to be in love all the time, but somehow our society has decided that this is an impossible state to maintain. "Real life" gets in the way, and we learn to settle for less. We wonder why everything inside us tells us otherwise and why we are all so addicted to watching other people fall in love in movies, TV, and music. We wonder why wars have been fought over love, kings have given up crowns, and people have taken their own lives.

Consider the possibility that you could be in love all the time, not just with a lover but with yourself, the world, and life itself. When you find love within yourself and realize that love is not dependent on another person, event, or degree of accomplishment, your world will change so dramatically you will wake each morning in amazement.

You can do this! As I mentioned, I like to do things the easy way with clear directions and have fun while I am doing it. If I can do it, so can you.

> Assume that everyone is madly in love with you!

Doing Too Much

I used to think that only I could do things "the right way." In reality, when I looked hard at myself, I had low expectations of the other people around me in order to feel good about myself. I've learned that people will rise and fall to my expectations, and if I have low expectations, they will meet them! To compensate, I used to kill myself trying to do everything. Do you do this? I've found that if you believe in people, you will find you have incredible support, and other people will start doing things quite well.

You also have to detach from having to be right, for there are many ways to do things, and your way is not the only way. You can't create a glorious life of joy, abundance, and love if you spend all of your energy being right because that takes a huge effort in the controlling and convincing of everyone around you. Relax, let go, and watch the magic in your life start happening on such a regular basis there will be no doubt in your mind that you are magnificent.

Who Do You Want to Be When You Grow Up?

Do you want to be a certain kind of person? This has nothing to do with doing anything. It's about being who you are. This is hard for many of us to accept because we were taught we aren't good enough as is and so we have to prove our worth by doing things.

It's not what people DO that makes them happy and successful. It's just the opposite. Happy and successful people have just allowed themselves to BE—to unfold into who they really are. It is when we force ourselves to follow a path because that is what we were told to do by someone else that we find ourselves dissatisfied and stressed.

All the doing in the world will not create a being. Who we are (our being) drives our actions (the doing).

For example, there is a woman who loves her work. Someone else would not suddenly become happy just by taking over her job. This woman's happiness is about how her work expresses her *being* and is not about a particular thing anyone else should be *doing*.

When you think you are limited, then you are "being" limited. As soon as you give yourself or someone else a label, you only experience the reality of that label until you choose differently.

I know a man who was attached to being "a man of his word." I asked him if he would stay in an unhappy marriage if he later met someone and fell in love. He said he would honor the marriage. I'm not making a judgment of right or wrong here, but for myself, I would not want to be with a man who was just honoring his agreement. I want to be with someone who loves me and is passionate.

Where is this man's connection to his truth? His decision to be a "man of his word" is really a judgment that he is better than others who are not, so he lives in the prison of a life not fully realized.

This is what happens when we use a label to hide behind and judge others, no matter how noble the label. I think honoring an agreement is a noble idea, but hiding behind a noble idea doesn't serve anyone in this picture. Agreements can always be revised and new agreements reached.

Keeping Our Energy Flowing

We need to connect to other people and keep our energy flowing in a healthy way, like a free flowing river. Instead, we dam ourselves up and throw stuff in the rivers of our lives. We clog the flow of energy and wonder why we can't see to the bottom and why no more water can get through.

I was having dinner with a young woman who was extremely focused on her job while working on her Master's degree. She was constantly in "doing" mode. She told me, "I could not stand myself if I wasn't doing something all the time." If she continues defining herself by what she *does*, she will really never *have* anything she truly wants. I should know—I've been there and done that. It may be that she is happy right now in the doing mode, but if she defines herself by doing, she is living in a house of cards that can easily be destroyed.

Many of us feel unworthy. We are constantly comparing ourselves to others. This is how we clog our own river of energy. To get your energy flowing, be yourself. Remove the comparisons and be who you are, not who you think you're supposed to be.

> Be yourself and follow your passion.
> Then all will be provided for you.

My brother recently called and complained about a "slacker" at his new job. He was irritated by this guy who never did his share and only worked when a supervisor was watching. My brother was expecting me to commiserate with him, but I didn't. I asked him if he enjoyed his work. He said yes. Maybe this slacker, I said, doesn't enjoy his work. Maybe he is fearful he will be fired, so he seeks approval when his supervisors are around. Imagine what it must be like living in his shoes: not liking the job, needing approval from someone else, and being fearful all the time. In contrast, bro, you are happy in your job, and the only problem you have is that you have chosen to be irritated by this guy's actions. I recommend that you choose again, unless you enjoy being irritated.

Some people seem to enjoy being sad, angry, stressed, upset, etc. I do not judge them because I know they have a choice to feel what they want. My stepson once asked, "What fun would life be if I can't have arguments and fights?" The beauty of life is that if you want an argument or whatever, the universe will supply you with it. In fact, the universe will supply you with whatever you want.

The problem is that most of us don't know what we want because we're too busy judging and labeling everybody and every action. This, of course, is not a "bad" thing, unless you want to have great joy and unbounded peace and love. Engaging in that kind of thought and belief doesn't make you less magnificent; it just prevents you from experiencing joy and love. I chose joy and love over anger and judgment, but that is my choice. I just want you to know that in every moment you make a choice whether on purpose or allowing your default program to choose it for you. If you want more fun and joy and ease, make deliberate choices to that end.

> To change your life dramatically, go through your day randomly smiling at people.

Wink at someone in a flirtatious way just for the fun of it. Sometimes I say hello to people or wave frantically to people I don't even know. It makes people feel good or at least wakes them up. I do this because it is fun, and I love doing it.

Personal Passion

This is the whole point: If it's not fun, don't do it. If you find that you are really not interested in helping the homeless, then don't help the homeless. If you find that you are really not interested in helping battered women, don't help battered women. If you find that your passion is helping children who don't have homes or trying to give children a better education, then do that. Maybe it is saving the whales; whatever it is, if that is your passion, then do it with passion and forget about the rest.

Someone else may be passionate about the things that don't interest you. If you are following other people's passions instead of your own, you may be blocking them from fulfilling their own purpose. So you are actually causing harm, not only to yourself, but to others as well. When you do what you aren't meant to do, you not only waste your precious life off purpose but you make it more difficult for others to be on purpose.

If you have little interest in a cause yet feel obligated to support that cause and spend your precious life moments at meetings and conferences and running errands for the cause, you are just running away from your true purpose. There is someone out there who wants that job that you are occupying, but because you are doing it, they can't find their way to doing it.

If you feel obligated to do something because there is no one else to do it, then maybe it isn't meant to be done. There may be no purpose to the action, or there may be a better way to get it done. If you don't do it, that particular action won't get done, or a better way will be found. The natural course of ending or evolution will take place. It is perfectly okay; nothing material or physical lasts forever, and that includes causes.

> When you are on purpose, everything else falls into place naturally.

Life becomes easier and completely clear when you turn towards the positive, pleasurable, and attractive and away from the negative, uncomfortable, and repulsive. Contrary to public opinion, if left to your own devices, you will not become a monster, or even worse, a lazy monster. I have found that, by following my heart's desire, I have become a glorious, unconditional, and unlimited loving being who derives more pleasure from life than I ever dreamed possible. I also manage to get more accomplished than ever before.

"Difficult" People and Whacks on the Head

If there is somebody in your life who you don't like, realize that they are there because you created them. An analogy might be to think of the world and your thoughts as a big computer. You are sitting there at this computer, creating your life. Up until now, you have been pressing some buttons but were unclear on cause and effect. Something whacks you on the head and you wonder, "Who did that?" You press a button again, and it whacks you on the head, and you keep trying to figure out, "Who did that?" Well, you did it.

Somehow you pressed the button that created the whack on the head. So when something happens in your life that you don't like or you are not happy with, don't blame others. You are the one pushing the buttons. You are to see yourself as a being just learning how to work the controls. Be patient, kind, and gentle with yourself about it all.

Perhaps you have given your computer (your power) away to someone else, and it is time to take it back. In other words, you are letting other people push your buttons. Once you recognize this, it is easier to stop or just remove the button completely by replacing it with a better button.

Realize that the whack on the head is a gift because now you have an opportunity to learn about that button. You might learn not to press it anymore or possibly even delete it or change its function. When you realize that you are the one who created the event and take responsibility for everything that happens in your life, you are in control. That does not mean you have to be controlling. There is a difference between being *in control* and being *controlling*.

Being controlling means you want everybody in your life to be what you think they should be in order to feed your own ego. *Being in control* is different. It means making your own choices. People that have control of their lives and their schedules are healthier and experience less stress. In fact, they did experiments on rats by shocking them. They found that the rats that could turn the shock off were healthier than the rats that could not turn it off, even though they were getting shocked the same number of times.

I am not recommending getting shocked or taking any "negative" processes and learning to enjoy them. In the process of learning how to create a better life, you may have to redefine some aspects of your life and see what silver linings they have.

You can take a lot of blows if you are choosing to take the blows and you have control over shutting them off. When you realize that you are in control of your life, you can also choose to continue what you have already created. You don't have to get rid of your father or change your job or divorce your husband or kick your kids out or whatever is upsetting you. No, it means that now you know you are taking the blows; there is a reason for it, and you get to *choose*. "Do I want to continue taking this particular blow? Is it worth it?"

You may actually find that "the blows" are really not negative now that you love yourself unconditionally, and it is ironic how redefining a behavior as it relates to you almost always eliminates the behavior that is undesirable.

Here is an example of this: At one point someone close to me in my life was what we would label verbally abusive. I could find many people who would agree that this behavior was "wrong," and no matter what I did, it continued until I stopped letting it affect me and realized that it was an indication of the other person's pain and disconnection from who they were. Once I did that, the behavior just stopped. I was amazed by this, and since then there have been many examples of that very same principal. It works every time.

In fact, if you redefine your whole life as something you have chosen, then the whole thing takes on a purpose that is sacred. It also gives you the power to make other choices.

You can eliminate *all* of the stress in your life. When you really love yourself unconditionally, you know who you really are. You know the truth of this life. You don't have any fears, and if you have no fears, you have no stress. When you know that God or the universal intelligence adores you, pure and simple, it's easier for you to love who you are and to know that everything is a gift. Then you can enjoy people more. There is so much more to learn, and every day we can become even more joyful and happy.

Infinite Ways to the Top of the Mountain

There are infinite ways to get to the top of the mountain. You can go up the hard way, you can go up the easy way, or you can follow the signs. There are many ways to go, and not every way is for every person. You already know the way even though it may be hidden. Don't let anyone else force you into his or her way, and don't allow yourself to follow the path that is not right for you. You will feel stressed if you do because, deep within you, "your way" is trying to get out in the open.

You are already the person who knows your own truth better than anyone else. Whatever you read, even this book, whatever you listen to, whatever health practitioner you see, whether a conventional doctor, a Reiki therapist, a massage therapist…realize that you need to weigh what is being said against *your own truth* and make sure that whatever you get from the interaction is your truth, not theirs.

Your truth is within you already, and you have chosen these vehicles to bring this knowledge to your awareness to let you know what you want to do with your life, how to go about it, and how to move on to the next step, whether it is becoming healthier, becoming more enlightened, becoming more joyful, becoming more peaceful, less stressed, thinner, or financially independent. Whatever it is that you are looking for, you know how to do it already. You actually know what to do, and you do not need any of us. We are here because you have asked for the information to come from outside yourself. At some point, you will no longer need to have information come from outside yourself.

The key is to find your own path. You are connected to infinite wisdom, but your doors may be shut. You can turn a dysfunctional life into an enlightened paradise without changing any external factors. Don't forget your path will always feel good and attract you.

Opening Your Doors, Changing Your Script

We live in little societies that have their own rules and rulers, and we become imprisoned and defined by them. These rules come from advertising, movies, your family, your work, and your community.

You cannot be controlled unless you allow it. Here you are, playing the role you were assigned or that you unconsciously assigned yourself. You are the mother, wife, father, husband, worker, boss, child, etc.

In our society, these roles come with their scripts. As you take on more and more roles, it gets harder and harder to juggle the scripts. Sometimes you forget your lines during your wife role while playing the mother role, and the father/husband misses his cue because he was confused by the wife's missed lines. And there are other "baggage" roles, such as abused child, unloved wife, unappreciated worker, etc., that add their own flavor to the drama.

> Be yourself. Follow your own ideas, guides, convictions, and passions.

Most of you have been indoctrinated to believe you must squash your desires because:

- Humans are inherently weak and bad and will trash themselves and their environment if allowed to do what they want.
- You must put in your time before you can reap the rewards.
- Sacrifices must be made.
- You shouldn't choose what you love but instead be practical and safe.
- You have to earn respect or things.
- You must listen to people who are in positions of authority.

With all these inner voices yelling at you, it's difficult to feel motivated to follow a passion (if you haven't already squashed it beyond recognition).

Simple Pleasures

I would suggest experimenting with simple pleasures. Get a massage or facial. Take a pottery class. Each step you take will lead you further. You might find out about Reiki therapy from your massage therapist and pursue that. You might learn you hate pottery but make a new friend at the class who steers you towards recording music or writing poetry. You might try a new attitude at work or incorporate a healing touch intention with each patron without letting them know. You might volunteer at a hospital and decide to get into the healing profession. Or you might realize that's not for you but that you have a passion for publicizing health awareness.

Whatever simple pleasure you are drawn to, even if it is doing nothing and relaxing, learn to cherish that moment and count it as just as important and worthy as any other moment. You may find the inspiration in that moment to do something that changes the world. In fact, there are some of us who believe that every time someone is in a happier state than that last moment, there are world changing effects. Hmmm, something to think about.

All of your life is an adventure into self.

When I began working on myself to change my experience of life, I was inspired to realize that every feeling I had was an opportunity to learn something about myself. I transformed struggle and pain into questions. "Hmmm…That person's trying to get a rise out of me. What do I get out of getting angry at this? What do I need to pay attention to or heal?"

I began to look forward to "negative" emotions so that I could learn more about where I had a leak of energy that I could repair. I was pleasantly surprised as I dealt with each episode of anger, sadness, hurt, or irritation and went inside myself to uncover my own insecurities, fears, judgments, or worn out beliefs. As I examined and changed my inner beliefs, I found the courage to choose joy, and my outer world transformed.

By the way, there is nothing I do regularly because I am supposed to do it. I don't follow a strict diet or avoid things because they are bad for me. I do what I love to do, moving toward what draws me and is passionate. I drink coffee, eat meat, and enjoy a cocktail. I nonetheless have reached a state of peace, joy, health, wealth, and incredible love and happiness. You can too!

Here's a summary of the key principles that have helped me get to this state.

How to Create a Life of Joy:

- Allow yourself to have the feelings you want independent of the circumstances that surround you.
- Assume that everyone is madly in love with you.
- Give yourself permission to feel loved from the inside, and you will create love all around you, drawing others to you who love themselves and are capable of loving you.
- Move toward joy, not away from it.
  - ‣ Spend time with only the people you enjoy.

- Do work that you love.
  - ‣ Success is not born of hard work.
  - ‣ Success is born of doing what you love.
- Make conscious choices.
  - ‣ Every person has the choice to be where he or she wants to be and has the capacity to choose something different to change the situations.
- Shift your beliefs.
- What you think you deserve and believe within yourself is what will happen.
  - ‣ However you imagine the process will be—easy or hard—is how it will be.
  - ‣ Fill your life with inspirational thinking.
- Learn how to have intense feelings about something without being attached to results or outcomes.
- Be yourself and follow your passion.
  - ‣ Your life is not just doing. It's about being.
- Realize that guilt and worry have no place in your perfect, magnificent being.

CHAPTER 2

Listen to Your Inner Voice

Iknow who you are, and you are wonderful beyond your most spectacular imaginings! You are magnificent beyond compare and have truly unlimited potential. Thinking in certain ways cuts you off from that reality. Your being is unlimited. You can do anything, including denying your truth. If you are not experiencing heaven on earth, then you're not living your truth. There is no limit to what amazing experiences are yours for the taking.

Hearing the Voice of God or the Divine

There is a voice within you that tells you how beautiful you are. There is a voice within you that tells you how lovable you are. There is a voice within you that lets you know you are perfect and protected. There is a voice within you that explains to you how much joy and love you contribute to the universe. There is a voice within you that, when you listen to it, stirs an emotion of such intense love that you feel tears well up in your eyes. Listen to it. It is the voice of God or the Divine.

Many of us have been brainwashed to believe that we must hear the Divine through someone or something else: a book or a church or the teachings of "sages."

However, the voice of God is inside YOU and everyone else. Outer pressures may have caused you to give up trying to hear this voice. Your inner voice is worth reclaiming. Otherwise, you will miss out on the wonderful experience of your life fully lived. There is no need to wander through life feeling constantly tired, angry, hurt, bored, guilty, frustrated, overwhelmed, or stressed only catching occasional glimpses of the true potential of life on earth. You can connect directly to your joy!

Learning to Listen Again

The voice of God sounds like this:

"You are my true love. I adore you and get such an incredible amount of joy from you—just watching you smile, the way you move, the things you say. Even when you think you've done something wrong, I know it was the best you could have done. It had to happen that way for all parties involved so you could each fulfill your purpose. You are still so beautiful. All of the flaws you think you have, I find absolutely wonderful and, at times, fascinating.

"I keep trying to give you the world, but you keep turning me down. It doesn't bother me except that you think you need to suffer before you can have it. You are already more than worthy, and I love you. Do you know how much I love you? Every moment of your existence, I send you more love than you can possibly imagine. Imagine a time when you felt very loved or very loving. Multiply that by the highest number you can think of or infinity if possible. That love energy is surrounding you at this moment.

It is a mother's love, a father's love, a lover's love, a friend's love, a child's love, and a love that cannot be described. When I look upon you, I am in as much awe as if I am looking at the ocean, a waterfall, or an incredible sunset.

"Look around you. Whatever beauty you see is my gift to you. There is so much beauty, and it is all for you. The flowers in spring–just for you. The sunrise and sunset–just for you. The ocean beaches–just for you. The blanket of snow–just for you. The smile of a small child in passing–just for you. The good-looking person that you just walked by–just for you. The tree lined streets–just for you. I give you the world and keep giving it to you because I love you so very much. You need do nothing because you are already perfect and perfectly loved."

These are the things you want to hear, aren't they? Start telling yourself all the things you want to hear. Whatever makes you feel joyous, thrilled, inspired, tell yourself that. Even if it sounds like you're making it up, say these things to yourself.

Ironically, most people expect that if you have these thoughts, if you say these things to yourself and believe them, you would go around being a lazy sloth or doing hurtful things, but the opposite is true.

When you realize you need do nothing to be loved, then you do what you want with love, and that starts a chain reaction of loving-kindness. When you feel perfect and perfectly loved, you have no desire to be hurtful. It is as simple as that.

Focusing on that inner voice is really important. It will guide you through every day. When you feel like you are lost or you don't have the energy that you need, just focus on this inner voice, and it will give you direction or give you an answer or reenergize you.

How Do You Get Your Inner Voice Back?

Pay attention to yourself, and for now, forget everyone else. If you are trying to control other people, you will be too busy and spending too much effort on that endeavor to hear this voice.

The voice may have gotten so small that you can't hear it over the other thoughts that crowd your mind. That's why you may turn to other sources, including this book, to be reminded of it and to hear it again. Your inner voice will find a way for you to hear it somehow, someday, no matter how hard you try to ignore it. So, quiet your thoughts and listen. If nothing comes, or if thoughts come up that make you feel less than overwhelming joy and love, be patient and say kind things to yourself.

If you start putting yourself down for not doing something you should have done, remember you need do nothing. If you feel remorse for something you did, remember that, if it happened, it had to happen, and you are still perfect and perfectly loved.

Get into the habit of having this loving voice reword any negative comments about you to you. As soon as you start getting on your own case, pretend you are the most adoring lover or doting parent, and give yourself unconditional love. Say the words in your mind as many times as it takes to make you feel good. Say the words out loud in private if you dare; that is powerful.

If you are having trouble figuring out what these adoring people might say because you never experienced someone treating you that way, take it from a movie or a poem. What I do is tell myself what I want to hear about me as if it were true. (It is true now.) I recreate for myself the most intense feelings I have had for others when I thought I was madly in love with them and they could do no wrong. When you are safe with this voice who loves you beyond compare, it will then be loud enough to help you in other areas of your life—relationships, business, body image, and even locating your keys. Just ask.

Remember, if the voice makes you feel anything less than loved, cherished, and absolutely wonderful, then it is not the right voice, not the voice of the divine. This is true no matter what you have done or not, "right" or "wrong." If you have hurt another, it will address your pain and try to fill your needs so you don't have to hurt again. It will never make you feel guilty or think less of you.

The Difference between Your Conscience and Your Inner Voice

Many of us think our conscience is the voice of God, but I am here to tell you it's not. It is neither a good or bad thing. Until you can connect to God's inner voice, your conscience allows you to function in your society in a relatively safe way. How your conscience guides you is a function of what you are taught and what you believe, and these things can be in error.

There have been societies that felt human sacrifice was good. There are religions now that advocate acts of terrorism. All of this has been done in "good conscience."

So when you hear your conscience, first go to the place where you feel unconditional love for yourself, and then listen again. You will find that the message may change. You will find your options expand, and you will not feel guilt or shame.

Some people are afraid that if people stopped feeling guilty for the things they do, the world would go down the tubes.

That is the thought of a person who wants to control others and does not believe in the inherent goodness of others. What you think of others is a reflection of what you think of yourself deep down. And how you think of others is often how they will act towards you. We are all connected. When you practice controlling others, it is because you have lost your own inner voice and fallen out of control. You will never have peace if you continue to think this way.

The world is full of self-fulfilling prophecies. If you start adopting everything you hear as your own belief, your life will continue as a self-fulfilling prophecy. People will take advantage of you if you believe they will. Listen to your inner voice, your connection to the divine, and you will create a better life, one that gives you greater joy than you can imagine.

The Inner Voice of Disease

Your inner voice can heal dis-ease. Your body actually responds when you talk to it. In a recent lecture by Dr. Wayne Dyer, he tells a story about his daughter.

"My daughter had a rash on her face, and it was supposed to be a kind of rash that goes away within six months on its own. She had it for FOUR YEARS, and it wasn't getting any better so I took her to a friend who was a dermatologist. My daughter had been to dermatologists before, but this doctor had an unconventional approach. He sat down with my 10-year-old and said, 'You need to talk to your rash and see what it has to say.'

"That night I found my daughter under the blanket with a flashlight talking to her rash. Believe it or not, this worked! The rash went away within three days."

I had a similar experience when I was 12. I had warts on my hands. My doctor burned one of them off and told me to wish the others away. I followed his advice, talked to my warts, and within two weeks they were gone.

The mind is a powerful thing, so talk to your illnesses. Ask questions like, "Why are you here? What do I have to learn from you? What am I focusing my attention on in error? What do I need to change?" You will probably gain insight, or someone will show up in your life and say, "You know what? I had the same problem. Here's what I did, and it went away." And then you say, "It's perfect that this person showed up at this time. I'll try what worked for them."

What works for another may not always work for you, but if you are listening closely or feeling clearly, you will be drawn to what will work for you. You will feel drawn to the right action or non-action because it feels good. If you are unsure, then continue working on being unconditionally loving to yourself, and the answer will come.

Messages from Life

That is how life works. You get answers from yourself, or you bump into somebody who gives you answers to your questions without you saying a word.

A woman I know had horrible back pain. She went to many doctors for help. Then one day she bumped into a friend she had not seen in years. While chatting, her friend noticed she was limping and asked about her back pain. This friend then recommended a physical therapist who she knew was very good. My friend recognized this was not a coincidence. It was a message for an action that she should take. She went to the physical therapist and was cured of her pain. So, pay attention to the messages that life sends you.

Inner Voice/Inner Diet

Listening to your inner voice has important applications in relation to the food we eat and the messages we give ourselves about eating pleasure. It's an area where we've been taught lots of confusing "should" and "should nots." But we can untangle these and find joy and health.

My brother is my inspiration in this area. He is participating in a "weight down diet" club. The philosophy is excellent: God made you perfect and did not mean for you to be overweight or unhealthy. God would never want that for you. The diet plan is to pay attention to the subtle signals that God gives you about what your body needs.

Participants are instructed to listen to that hungry feeling that they get; it tells the person that they need to eat and to eat certain foods.

They are told to "Only eat when you are hungry." Most of us eat because we are trying to get some sort of relief or trying to medicate a depression or we are bored. To live a joyful life, EAT when you are hungry, and EAT CHOCOLATE if you feel like eating chocolate. You will find that if you follow your desires, you will eat when you are hungry, and you will eat what you want. You will start craving only things that our body really needs.

Your body will tell you what you need. Let's say you keep eating chocolate for two weeks in a row, and all of a sudden you think, "I'm really not in the mood for chocolate anymore. I could have it, but I don't feel like it. I think I am going to have a salad and put a little bacon on it."

Certainly there is a reason for the failure rate of diet programs, and the reason is because people try to lose weight through doing something such as diet and exercise. In truth, without changing your **mind** about your weight, your relationship with food, and ultimately yourself and your connection to your divine inner being, no regimen will work long term.

Stop trying and just start enjoying life and yourself. Imagine how it would feel to be as you desire and walk through life as if it is. In every moment, love yourself as much as possible and know that love surrounds you always.

Trust Yourself

You will choose the right things. You were taught that you must go against your feelings and keep yourself from those things that you love.

Listen to yourself. Trust yourself, and don't be hung up on low fat food or the going trends. After all, they change the nutrition rules every 10 years. At one time we were told that eggs were very healthy; then they weren't. Now they are "healthy" again.

Lastly, the most important thing in weight loss is to regain your joy and passion. If you are passionate about your life, you will eat less and do more. There is no incentive to be thin and healthy if you aren't going to use your thin, healthy body for joyful and pleasurable activities.

Follow your intuition; follow the inner voice. It will tell you what you need to do in your relationships, it will tell you how to heal your illnesses, and it will help you eat for health and joy.

CHAPTER 3

Take Back Your Power

Living a life of joy means you need to claim *all* of your power. I've learned to do this. You can too! Most of us have given a lot of our power away for a long time. You may have been taught to give it up to other people or institutions, to anyone in a position of authority. It's time to reclaim your own authority.

Here are the four keys to my power (and yours):

1. Acknowledge and draw on your own infinite supply of love and energy. (We all have access to the same supplier.)
2. Plug up your own energy leaks. Deactivate your hot buttons.
3. Refrain from stealing energy from anyone else.
4. Be generous from your spiritually secure self.

> "There is an infinite source of energy called Love. It is available to anyone directly from the source and it is not necessary to take it from other people." (From The Celestine Prophecy)

Key #1: Acknowledge and Draw Upon Your Own Infinite Supply of Love and Energy

Do you know that you have access to an infinite source of energy? It is the source of all creation, and you have a direct pipeline to it. You don't have to go through anyone or anything else to get it. It is your birthright, your connection to God and the universe. To tap into it requires that you develop unconditional love for yourself, that you cultivate awe of and appreciation for what you have been given, and that you learn to be present in the moment.

You can do this without quitting your job, divorcing your spouse, giving your children up for adoption, or joining a monastery in China (unless, of course, that is what you want to do). Learning how to fill yourself up from this infinite source of energy is so freeing and energizing that it becomes habit forming and builds on itself.

Pay Attention

Start by paying attention to the beauty around you in whatever form it takes, man-made or natural. Receive it as a gift from God. It actually is, but if you don't yet know this to be true, pretend that it is anyway. This pretending (imagining, appreciating, dreaming it up) is how you create your world the way you want it.

I used to drive around in my car, totally preoccupied mentally with have-to-dos and should-have-dones. One day I decided to actually NOTICE my world. I looked up at the sky and was AMAZED at the ongoing beauty of the clouds. (Why do we only appreciate these things when they are surrounded by a frame and hung on a wall in a museum?)

Around the same time, I realized that I had been driving by the same farmland for years and never noticed that someone had put up special birdhouses to attract bluebirds. As I drove through the area, I noticed these incredible creatures. Again, I was struck by beauty that had been there all along (but not in my awareness, which was tied up in mental traffic).

Just so I would get the point, another miracle of awareness happened. *A hawk flew up to my window and then perched on the railing of my deck.* "See," it seemed to say, "there are rewards for noticing, for paying attention and appreciating the power and beauty all around you."

So, the first step in accepting your unlimited supply of love and energy is just to notice how you are constantly surrounded by it already.

Fill Yourself with Love

The second step, as we discussed in the first chapter, is to intentionally fill yourself with the feeling of love. This is how you tap into your unlimited supply of love and energy. It is your own responsibility to do this. If you have the false idea that someone else can make you happy, then you must also live with the reality that someone else can make you *unhappy*.

If you take care of filling yourself up, then you will always have an infinite supply of joy.

The irony is that when you activate your own infinite source, people will flock to you to give you more. On some level, people sense that you have no clinging needs or hidden agendas and find it safe to give you more love and energy.

Key #2: Plug Up Your Own Energy Leaks

Are you aware of how much of your energy you give away? Once you learn to plug up your energy leaks and stop giving away what you need and deserve for yourself, you will be amazed at how much energy and joy you have. Everyone has access to all the energy they need, including you. No one needs to take energy from another, yet we often try to do so. Accepting how amazing you already are allows you to master the dance of life and escape this harmful dynamic. Learning to be aware of how and why you give your energy away is essential to creating the life of abundance that you desire.

Deactivate Your Hot Buttons

How often have you given away your energy to someone else? Did you scream at someone when they cut you off in traffic? Did you get flustered when someone else criticized you? Were you so impressed with someone else that you put them on a pedestal and felt less valuable yourself?

Identify Your Energy Leaks

The key here is to recognize your own outlay of energy and become aware of where and to whom you are giving it.

Then you can begin to understand why you give it away. The cause is usually fear or insecurity. Once you deal directly with that fear, insecurity, or limiting belief, you will no longer give energy to the petty tyrants or "energy vampires" in your life.

Energy Suckers

Some people suck your energy by being insulting or physically abusive toward you. The flip side of this kind of energy sucker is the martyr who takes your energy by acting like a helpless victim who must be taken care of. Both of these energy suckers are your greatest teachers because they show you where you are a leaky vessel and where you need to change your beliefs.

How to Get Rid of Energy Suckers

Once you shift your beliefs and get rid of your fears, energy-draining people will either change their behavior around you or leave your presence altogether. This has been my experience. As they fail in their attempts to drain you, you will no longer be a target because you are no longer a source of energy-on-demand for these people. They may continue to drain the life out of others, but they will give up trying to drain *you* because they can't.

The Dance of Life

Life is a lot about energy. The love that I talk about all through this book, this feeling of love, is actually energy. You are inspired to do many things when you are in love, and you have boundless energy to do them. When you are involved in a passionate activity, you have an infinite amount of energy and don't feel tired. Those feelings stimulate and motivate you.

We are all looking for energy and love. Until we learn to go directly to the source for it, we try to take energy from each other.

Dancing the Two-Step

- **Step One:** Someone comes up to you in an angry way.
- **Step Two:** You react and give them your energy. They just suck it out of you.

When you are around certain people, whether they are actively or passively aggressive, you feel drained. They may be very critical, and you always feel on edge around them and can't seem to do anything right. Or they may constantly fall apart and tug on you for help. These people are draining you of your energy, and you are allowing it. It is important to realize that you are allowing them to drain your energy.

Changing the Dance

A colleague of mine once said to me in anger "You don't do %&#* around here!" and I replied, "Yes, isn't it great?" I had disengaged my sense of self-worth from my accomplishments! This freed me to pursue what I really wanted to do, what I was passionate about. I became more productive by doing what was meaningful to me. This, in turn, gave my life purpose and balance.

My colleague didn't like it that way. He was attached to me being the one who did those specific actions in spite of the fact that all of it was getting done, and I arranged it and paid for it, and there was no downside to his experience. He couldn't see outside the box and just be happy.

This no longer affected me, so he stopped trying to change me. Eventually, we parted company. I am sure he will find someone who he can control for a while and continue this pattern until he wakes up. Someone who needs this experience will fall into it with him, and the dance will continue until one of them wakes up or wants another kind of dance.

How to Protect Yourself

I followed a series of steps as I learned to protect myself from having my energy drained by other people. The first thing I did was to pay attention and identify the energy-draining dances (strategies) of people around me. After I observed and identified the dance, I removed myself from the other person's influence and stopped my energy from leaking by examining and deactivating the underlying belief I carried that made me vulnerable to that person.

When my energy is leaking, I recognize that the other person in the interaction is not to blame. I am losing energy because I *already have a leak caused by a false belief.* For example, if someone is telling me that somehow I'm "not good enough," he or she will only get energy from me if I too believe this on some level and go along with criticizing myself.

Turning around and directing the same false idea at the other person doesn't work either. Even if I could find a thousand people to agree with me that this other guy is a jerk and deserves my anger, this is not the case. If I vent my anger at him, I am giving away my energy, and I am responsible for that.

Super Button-Pushers

Some people are really good at pushing your buttons and getting you to react. It is in YOUR power to become aware of your buttons and deactivate them. Then you will stop losing energy. In fact, you should be thanking the "jerk" for showing you where you have a button to push.

The hardest button-pushers to handle, of course, are the people you love. If someone else that you had no emotional investment in did the same thing as your loved one, it wouldn't bother you. But you have an idea that a person should act in a certain way because she/he is your lover, spouse, best friend, child, etc.

No matter who annoys, angers, or grieves you, take responsibility for your energy loss and all your hot buttons. Realize that you always have a choice in how you react to any given situation. This is a concept that requires application 100% of the time. You can't make an exception and say certain behaviors justify a negative choice and some don't. Even if someone caused you great loss, there is always a loving, positive choice available. It may take a while to be able to notice that you have more than one choice in this kind of situation, but you always do.

At the beginning of this path of awareness, you may find that you keep choosing the same negative response to certain behaviors. There is nothing wrong with this—you can continue to make this choice. However, if you want to expand your choices, if you want to change how you spend every moment of your life and make it magical, use that negative reaction as education for the future.

Knee-Jerk Reactions

Sometimes the choice will seem like a reflex that you have no control over. As soon as someone, such as your spouse, does a certain thing, you see red or feel hurt before you can even think. This is *still* a choice based on many subconscious beliefs and desires.

As you become more unconditionally loving of yourself and, of course, others—that goes hand in hand—you will find the beliefs within you that are holding you hostage. It is much like peeling an onion, layer after layer. Be patient with yourself and treat this like an adventure because it is—the most incredible and rewarding adventure of your life.

You will find that as you feel the negative emotion and immediately recognize it for the educational tool that it is, you will be able to turn your attention to yourself and where you need to uproot beliefs that hold you back.

This became a moment to moment exercise for me, but with my newfound knowledge, every negative emotion became an adventure into self and freedom.

I owned every experience without blaming myself or anyone else but claiming total responsibility and went on a journey to explore why I would choose to feel the way I felt. In the beginning, it was hit or miss finding the limiting belief that was responsible for creating the event and the feeling, but as I became more unconditionally loving of myself, I was able to figure it out most of the time.

Getting rid of the limiting belief was sometimes as easy as identifying it, and other times the roots were so deep and pervasive that I still have to go uproot them from time to time. Like weeds in a garden, sometimes just living in our world and being exposed to others and media throws a weed into our garden that takes root quickly unless we are caring for the garden of our lives daily and often.

Let's say that someone brags about their children and the accomplishments they have. Many of us would be unaffected by that, but if inside of you there was a belief that you weren't doing enough for your kids, you might feel inadequate or annoyed by this. In the moment that you felt that negative emotion, you would look inside and notice limiting beliefs within you about parenting and children.

All children are powerful beings who can accomplish anything in life with or without us. From their broader spiritual aspect, they chose to come into this world as your child and knew what they were getting into. Anything you can do for them is less important than showing them the example of a happy, self-actualized being. All is well, and your children are powerful unlimited spectacular beings.

Once you reassert your true belief over the old one, the feeling subsides, and you can actually enjoy the success of another without feelings of jealousy, inadequacy, or annoyance. You will also find that the parents who brag about their children do not come into your awareness anymore.

> Somewhere deep inside you there is a need to control other people's behavior so you can believe they love you or respect you.

Your mind may have a million preprogrammed ideas about how the other person is supposed to be. Your job at this point is to start becoming aware of your reactions to people and entertain the idea that all your reactions come from you, your beliefs, and your insecurities.

At the same time, you must become aware of how you have learned to steal energy from other people and stop doing it!

Key #3: Don't Steal Energy from Anyone Else

Your own energy-draining behavior stems from the same limiting beliefs that allow you to GIVE your energy away. No one is "less than" or "more than" another, and there is no need to deplete each other in order to have "enough." Remember, we all have our own access to an infinite supply of love and energy. We are all perfect eternal beings ALREADY.

When you are in a "bad mood" and use it to intimidate someone, you are taking energy from them. When you have negative feelings about someone you are with, that feeling is communicated without words. If you are communicating negative energy to others, then you are communicating a need that is asking to be filled at someone else's expense. If it is not filled, then you leave yourself open to disease or disaster.

Are you trying to get what you need in a certain way from a certain person? Are you being passive-aggressive with your kindness, obligating people to reciprocate? Are you limiting yourself by having too narrow a view and too judgmental an attitude?

Who "Should" Support You?

A patient of mine was just finishing chemotherapy for breast cancer. For the most part, she had a very enlightened attitude about her experience. However, she was complaining about how her husband was distant, uninvolved, and just plain not there for her.

She was very angry about this. Her sister, however, had given her solid support through this experience. I asked her why she felt her husband was responsible for "being there" or supporting her? Who made this rule up? Some people are incapable of dealing with other people's illnesses, and you may find yourself attached to someone like that.

There are no obligations in life that are set in stone.

This idea that her husband should be the one to "be there" was not serving her. This idea seemed more painful than her cancer treatments. She was receiving excellent support from her sister. I asked her why this wasn't good enough and how much support did she actually need?

After I asked these questions, I felt a twinge of guilt. Had I overstepped my bounds? In spite of this, we ended the appointment on a positive note with a hug. Weeks later, this woman came to a workshop I was giving and shared an amazing development with me. When she went home, she apologized to her husband for placing the burden and responsibility for her happiness, support, and wellbeing on him and released him from any expectation or obligation to carry this "burden." She realized that before she met him she was capable of being happy and taking care of herself and that this was still her own responsibility.

As a result of taking responsibility for herself, my patient no longer felt angry at her husband. She released herself from negative feelings she had taken on when she put expectations on her husband that he was not capable of filling. The added bonus was that, after that conversation, her husband changed his behavior, and their relationship improved. Now that she no longer expected him to be caring and supportive, he became just that!

Realizing Expectations

Each relationship has its own dynamics. To expect someone to be who they aren't is not only ineffective but potentially dangerous. You will probably not succeed and then have to live with the chronic negativity you create. Worse yet, if you do succeed in getting the other person to do what you want against his or her will, the other person will resent you and end up living a lie to avoid your wrath. Is that what you want?

You may want a supportive person in your life, but does it necessarily have to be your spouse? Make sure you are clear about your priorities. I would much rather have my sister be my support and my significant other be someone who rocks my world. I have plenty of great friends to call upon if I am ill. The man in my life is quite supportive, but I would rather reserve him for passion and intimacy. If I had to choose one or the other, I would opt to have passion with him and leave the support to my girlfriends. As always, when you don't need something but desire it with playful excitement, it becomes your reality. My partner in life is both passionate and supportive.

It is fascinating that when you no longer make demands of the people in your life, they seem to provide you with more than you need. In other words, when you don't *need* your spouse or lover to be supportive, they are. When you open your eyes to the fact that everything you want is already provided for you, more than you dreamed possible is given you. You always have what you want and need if you are open to accepting it and don't narrow your vision.

Many of us try to make our spouses responsible for everything in our lives even though many of our needs are already met by other relatives and friends. We complain and blame our significant others for the inadequacies in our lives. We ignore all of the wonderful things they do and instead complain about the things we are trying to control.

There is a sea of people just waiting to handle your every wish and desire as soon as you start to handle your own. Infinitely supplying yourself with love or energy on an ongoing basis attracts all that you want into your life as if by magic. You don't have to believe me, but this idea costs nothing to implement, and you will see it happen before your eyes.

Giving Up the Struggle

As you practice taking responsibility for your energy and your reactions, your life becomes less of a struggle and more of an adventure. Even though you may not make incredibly profound and loving choices immediately in the face of every situation, you are starting to interpret every negative reaction and situation as a part of your education. Instead of being sucked into emotion, you recognize it and pay attention to it, and then you look into yourself for the source of it.

You may not always find it right away, but every time you do, it will be easier and the answers clearer. Many times just coming up with the real reason you are angry instead of what you are telling yourself is the reason dissipates the anger immediately, and you are rid of that button forever.

Examples from the Operating Room of My Life

Getting control of my energy, both giving and receiving, has been an essential element for creating my "heaven on earth"—a life free of struggle and stress. Here are a few examples of how I did this:

My Spouse: I am divorced now, but at the time of this story, I was married to a man who got very angry when I had to work late. I felt like I owed my life to my work for many reasons. The operating room seemed to have no concern for my personal life. Actually, as I mentioned earlier, this is no longer the case for me, but at that time, I felt out of control in relation to my time.

This made my husband extremely angry, and he was verbally nasty to me. I responded by getting angry back at him, being insulted, and acting hurt. We argued. I cried. I used the cold shoulder method; I appealed to his love for me and was hurt by his lack of sensitivity to my needs. In other words, I was using socially sanctioned manipulation methods to attempt to change this behavior. It is hard to believe that grown people with medical degrees can act this way!

My position was that I was a surgeon before he married me, and he knew what he was getting into. Therefore, he had no right to be angry with me now. His position was that I was late on purpose, and I didn't care about his needs. There was no middle ground. This interaction was sapping my energy and making it unpleasant to even go home at night.

I decided to take responsibility for the situation and apply my newfound tools. I looked in the mirror and asked myself, "Why am I attracting this into my life?" and "Why do I choose to be upset and stressed about this?"

I saw that I was attached to being perfect. No matter how hard I tried, my husband told me I was a not a perfect wife as I interpreted it. Now I am thankful for that because it showed me that I was attached to someone else's opinion of me. My actions were for the purpose of getting that approval and not based in love and joy.

> He wouldn't let me be perfect.

When I could see how attached I was to an external, unrealistic idea of perfection, I realized where my leak of energy was. As long as I had that leak, other people could take energy from me by telling me how imperfect I was in one way or another.

Once I recognized this, I Immediately detached my ego from being defined by someone else's idea of perfection. By this time I had done enough reading and studying to know that perfection is just a concept. It doesn't exist in real life. On the other hand, we are already perfectly who we are at all times.

> I decided to love and honor myself no matter what I did or didn't do.

I decided that my feelings about myself would be attached to nothing but my own opinion of myself and that I adored me (not just liked but really ADORED me). When I did this, I began to see my husband's anger as a demonstration of his own inner pain. He couldn't see this yet. He continued to blame me for the discomfort in his life. I no longer felt offended or hurt by his anger. I calmly removed myself from taking responsibility for his experience.

My only concern was to be joyful in spite of his anger and criticism. I couldn't change his anger or his need to criticize.

> By changing myself, I changed the dynamics of our relationship.

This was a miraculous and surprising byproduct of changing myself. When, in my heart of hearts, I was no longer affected by my husband's anger and criticism and was able to acknowledge his pain, he stopped being angry and critical.

When you see clearly what is going on, you can stop being affected by the attempts of people to suck the life out of you. When you are truly unaffected by their anger and attempts to take your energy, they stop trying and go looking for someone else to drain. Or they begin to change as well and start taking responsibility for their own lives.

Of course, you cannot count on another person changing his or her attitude or actions. Luckily, you don't have to.

Your happiness and peace of mind are not contingent on anyone else changing his or her behavior.

By taking responsibility for my experience with my husband, I was able to rid myself of daily stress and anxiety. I was relieved at not being dragged into conflict and anger. I just let him be angry without me. Soon he stopped being angry with me because he saw that it got him nowhere.

To review, here are the steps I used and that YOU can use to "plug your leaks":

1. Notice where your energy is habitually leaking or being drained by someone else.
2. Examine yourself to find the belief ("hot" button) that makes you vulnerable to someone else taking your energy.
3. Plug the leak by deactivating the button (i.e., let go of your *need* for this belief).

Business: As with my husband, I found the same kinds of energy leaks happening in my business and was able to apply the same process.

I repeatedly had to deal with one of my partners in an adversarial way every time we approached a major issue for the business in our quarterly meetings. I would often get my way but with much angst and pre-meeting stress. I finally took responsibility for attracting this circumstance into my life and realized that it was my need to be right that attracted this conflict. I decided that I no longer needed my ego to be fed by this drama, and I let it go.

> I decided I didn't always have to be "right."

At the next meeting, there was a touchy issue on the agenda. People asked me if I was putting on my boxing gloves to deal with it. I simply stated that it would be different this time. I didn't know how it would be different, but I knew I no longer needed to be right. I no longer needed this drama to validate my self-worth. When the issue came up at the meeting, I stated what I thought should happen. Not only did my "adversary" agree with me, he had an idea that made it more attractive for everyone else!

In taking responsibility for the conflict, looking at the core idea behind my need for the experience, and then letting go of that need, I was able to get rid of a good bit of busywork and stress. This also allowed the members of my company to benefit from a good idea and enjoy the meeting. I no longer had to spend time planning my strategy for winning. Instead, I spent that time enjoying my life, my children, and my patients as well as experiencing the win-win of a truly successful business.

My Husband's Ex-Wife: My husband's ex-wife was another major problem in my life, and I blamed her for the whole thing. SHE was the problem, I was sure. Not ME.

I thought she lied about me to the kids. She didn't show up when she said she would. She did all kinds of things I disapproved of, and still her kids (my step kids) idolized her. I could find a thousand things about her to justify my self-righteous anger, and it was easy to get other people to agree with me about how bad she was. She was the one, after all, who left her children and her husband. Of course, cultivating other people's judgment about her only kept me more upset and justified in feeling that way.

Every time she came into the house, I felt anxious and angry. I took great care not to say anything nasty about her to the children so that I could believe I was doing the right thing. I saw myself as the ultimate martyr and kept my anxiety and animosity to myself around the house. Kids have great emotional radar, however, and even if I wasn't saying it or acting it, they knew how I felt because they could read my mind and body language.

I was with my stepchildren every day and just the mention of how great "mom" could cook would send a cascade of negative emotions through me. I wanted to shout, "If she is such a good cook, then why isn't she here cooking?" Of course, I didn't do this, but the children picked up on it and seemed to even enjoy my discomfort. After all, they were in pain with the loss of their mother, and I was the one THEY blamed.

This situation was a daily drain on my energy, so it was one of the first areas I decided to work on as I began to take responsibility for my feelings.

I asked myself, "Why do I get disturbed by her presence? Why am I upset by the love her children have for her?" When I examined her actions towards me, I realized that none of them would bother me from anyone else.

My next step was to look in the mirror of truth to see what really bothered me about his woman. It boiled down to the fact that she works out every day, and she can wear a thong bikini. I could tell this was the core problem because I had the strongest reaction to it. Looking directly at it allowed me to work through my issues with her and let go of my anger.

The other thing that bothered me was that all those years she was married to my husband she did everything I would have loved to do—went to the islands and had nice things, such as furs, jewels, and upscale cars. She never went to college and never had "to work" for these things while I had been busting my butt to become a surgeon. Again, I was jealous.

I realized that all of my negative feelings about her were really negative feelings about where I thought my life was lacking and had nothing to do with her.

I didn't feel like I was in good shape, and I didn't have fun vacations and nice things. I had to face the choices I had made. I decided to be a surgeon. She didn't make me become a surgeon. I decided not to work out every day. She didn't make me avoid working out.

I was using noble excuses for my negative feelings (about what she "did" to the children and my husband) to cover up my real feelings of jealousy. I couldn't even admit this to myself until I started to be unconditionally loving toward myself.

Once I acknowledged my jealousy and the core belief behind it ("I'm not good enough"), I easily released that anger and found that I could now send my husband's ex-wife positive thoughts and feel genuinely warm toward her. I noticed that she really was not a bad person but a genuinely good person. I realized that I was cutting her out because of my animosity to her. I was actually making her look worse to her kids by being the "best" or most perfect mother I could possibly be. It was strenuous trying to be Miss Perfect. And it was detracting from my relationship with my own son. I felt I had to put more time into my stepchildren because they were more "difficult" and causing me more pain.

When I could release my jealousy and judgments about my husband's ex-wife, I was able to share my life with her, my stepchildren and my son with happiness and joy instead of anxiety and animosity. I sent her a letter to make peace, and now we get along very well. I started calling her and welcoming her involvement with her kids, and you know what? They were much happier with their mother no matter what she did or didn't do. Children are the great unconditional lovers of all time. They were much happier with her doing her thing, her way, than with me doing it the way it was "supposed to be done."

In reality, there are no valid rules about how it is supposed to be done and so many imposed rules that have no basis in reality. The children wanted their mom to be herself, not me. The more I tried to be a good mother to them, the more animosity I experienced from them.

Being Okay with Being Imperfect

I was fascinated, not jealous or upset now. I learned so much through this experience. You see, any negative emotion can be used as a learning tool. I was learning to love myself in spite of my flaws. I could actually look in the mirror of truth, see something really petty about myself, accept it, let it go, and move on.

Anytime you feel anger, jealousy, animosity, or blame toward someone else, you must look at yourself more closely.

> Until you can see your part in this dance,
> you will be losing energy.

Your part may be simply sending out judgmental thoughts or having erroneous, outdated beliefs within you that still control your behavior and feelings. Finding your internal cause and cleaning it up actually gives you so much more time and energy. By clearing one area, I was able to allow my stepchildren to have a relationship with their mother without any overtones of animosity, spend more time with my own son, and rid myself of a daily drain of energy and emotion.

Key #4: Be Generous from Your Spiritually Secure Self

The more you practice identifying and releasing your limiting beliefs, the easier it becomes to have clear energy exchanges with other people. You get good at noticing when there is an energy drain in either direction and at making a decision to shift it.

As you get comfortable with this process, you find you have many more choices in your interactions. You don't have to be bound by old knee-jerk reactions. You are no longer a victim to anyone else sucking your energy because you know you have an infinite supply.

Now you can choose to give energy away when you feel like it, even to "energy vampires." You can give them all that they seek in ways that astound them. In doing this, you may sow seeds for their future transformation.

Someone who gives energy freely usually disconcerts people who seek to take it uninvited. Ironically, those people don't recognize the energy you give because they are so narrowly focused on getting it the way they usually get it. Energy vampires may be intimidated or turned off by you and avoid you. Because now you are no longer in need of their approval, this causes you no concern. In fact, you may prefer it. You have no leaks in your energy vessel to attract vampires.

Dealing with "Rude" People

If you find yourself angry at someone for being rude to you, give yourself some love and realize you don't need anyone else to be courteous for you to feel love, feel good, and feel absolutely enamored with life.

Now you can look at this "rude" person with compassion. This person must be in pain and in need of love in order to act this way. If you choose to, you can smile and shower them with the radiant love of your new awareness. They may be uplifted, disconcerted, or relieved. You know deep within yourself that, whether they acknowledge it or not, your gift of energy affects them. Like a ripple in the water, you have changed their world.

Compassion Even Works in Traffic Jams!

Try assuming that someone cutting you off in traffic is on the way to see a loved one at the hospital. Notice that you don't *have* to get upset or give energy to their aggressive driving. You can even beam love and kindness. Whether or not they notice it, you are able to keep your sense of joy and peace. And maybe some of it *will* rub off on them.

Extreme Cases

Even in the face of horrible injustices such as murder or rape, you can still be responsible for a loving reaction. (This does not exclude allowing that person to experience the consequences of the action, such as going to jail.) There will come a time when you genuinely have no anger at someone who is in so much pain that they chose to kill someone else. There will also come a time when you may feel genuine love for that person. You will have no attachment to the consequences of their actions and therefore no negative residue. In many cases, our anger is actually our own guilt about not having prevented something bad from happening. In fact, having negative emotions in response to "bad" things that happen increases the presence of these "bad" things in our world, but that is for another book.

I had a friend who was raped in her teens. After about ten years of subconsciously dealing with this burden, she was finally able to let it go. She realized the residue from the rape was that she was angry at herself! While she was growing up, she was taught that being a sensual woman was a bad thing and that wearing provocative clothing was the cause of rape in some cases. When it happened to her, she subconsciously blamed herself. This feeling of guilt and self-blame is what really plagued her. When she became aware of this, she could let it go. She celebrated her sensuality and released her guilt. The rape is no longer a charged event, and she is able to fully enjoy her life.

The Antidote to Pain Is Inside of You

Whenever you feel pain or seem to be repeatedly attracting the same bad experiences, you carry the antidote within you. The source of the feeling is within you, and the ability to change it is also within you. There are no exceptions to this. You have made the choice on some level to have this reaction or feeling. Take full responsibility; stop blaming anyone else. This doesn't mean that another person is always right or that you must continue being around that person. There are times when it is appropriate to have less contact with someone who "causes" you negative emotions and you are not yet able to stop your reaction.

Be Kind to Yourself

Often the person who is cruelest to you is your very own self. Being kind to yourself is essential to taking back your power. Stop putting yourself down! You are a glorious, magnificent creation. And one of the best things about you is that you have the power to create a great life for yourself. You have a choice to tap into the love that surrounds you. You get to choose how you give and receive energy, to choose what beliefs serve you and what beliefs to let go of. You get to choose joy as your way of being.

CHAPTER 4

Live in Beauty and Gratitude

I used to wake up reluctantly, feeling anxious and stressed all day long. This changed when I decided to follow this principle:

> Look for beauty, and be grateful for it everywhere you find it.

My whole life changed when I started doing this. When I decided to look for and appreciate the beauty in my world, I was astonished to find myself living in a new neighborhood. The funny thing was that I hadn't moved anywhere! I could find something inspiring to look at even in our old industrial park. A river runs through it, and the vistas as you drive across one small bridge or another are truly breathtaking. Of course, as I began appreciating everything, my children thought I had lost my mind. In truth I had finally found it.

I began to see beauty not only in my environment but in the people I encountered. There were so many previously unnoticed treasures in the people around me. I had to slow down a little to notice them.

The clerk in the store was so kind. The woman getting out of her car had beautiful hair. One of my colleagues had a fabulous, infectious laugh. I cultivated the habit of finding things in people or my environment to be grateful for, and I still often feel full of awe.

Before and After

A day in my life before I started applying these ideas would go like this: I woke up in the morning tired and reluctant to get out of bed, already thinking about what was in store for me during the day. I already felt guilty about not getting my chart work finished yesterday, not working out, not going over my children's homework, not spending more time with them, not reading the article I wanted to read, and not using all of my talents to become more successful.

After reviewing all these worries and woes, I would turn my thoughts to my spouse and how he wasn't living up to my dream of what a spouse should be. I dredged up recent arguments and went over the flaws in his character. I blamed him for my inability to engage in activities that I loved. If only he would be supportive of everything I wanted to do and not get angry! By now, my mind was in overdrive and I felt anxious, worried, and angry before I even got out of bed.

Next I would go to the bathroom to take a shower and start an inventory of my personal physical disasters. "Gray hair is starting to show. Where did that cellulite come from? My butt is too big, my breasts are too small, I should be working out more…" While I was busy criticizing myself, I was also rushing so I could get downstairs to wrestle with preparing lunches and getting the kids ready for school.

Do you recognize a little bit of yourself in this? Do you see how incredibly draining these negative thoughts are?

I think you get the picture, but wait! There's more.

Once I reached the kitchen, I was thrust into the struggle to get the kids to school and deal with their acting-out behavior, lost or forgotten homework, etc. Meanwhile, I was working myself up about what my workday had in store for me. I worried about all the difficult patients, hostile colleagues, delays in the operating room, and annoying problems that would fill my day.

I managed to get through the day only to come home to more conflict. I seemed to have no space or time for myself and, in fact, didn't even have time to really notice how miserable I was. I'd spend the evening driving kids here or there, getting last minute items for school or going to meetings. On the few evenings we did have dinner as a family, someone was always complaining and grumbling.

When I went to bed, I laid awake obsessing over the same negative thoughts that began my day. I finally settled down, but I never really rested deeply. I knew it would start all over again in the morning.

Change the Picture

Now my life is very different. I wake up in the morning relaxed and look forward to getting out of bed. I notice how the sun shines so beautifully through the windows and what a beautiful pattern the trees make against the wall. I feel the sheets touching my body and notice what a pleasurable sensation it is. I enjoy the artwork and trinkets in my room. I look in the mirror and pay attention to only those things I love about me and ignore any flaws. I express silent thanks for all of these things as I go along. When I get into the shower, I enjoy the feel of the hot water against my body and the gentle massage I am getting. I enjoy the feeling of the towel as I dry myself and the color and texture of my clothes as I put them on.

Taking My Time

I get ready for my day as if I have all the time in the world. I have come to realize that—

> I can only be in one place at a time doing one thing at a time in this physical world.

If you really think about it, what is the worst thing that can happen if you don't get the kids to school or you don't get to work on time? None of the consequences are life-threatening. However, living with stress is. So I make the logical choice to relax. Now I stay completely relaxed in all circumstances.

The children seem to act out less, and I give them the responsibility to get their own stuff together. I am available to help them if they ask nicely and allow enough time. Otherwise, I let them deal with consequences for their choices.

I can only be in one place at a time doing one thing at a time in this physical world.

> I no longer try to compensate for the effects of other people's choices.

I notice that as I take care of myself in this area, so do my children.

I request that everyone be positive and friendly in the car and only offer constructive criticism if warranted. Problems can be discussed in a positive and calm way or saved for another time. The car ride to school is pleasant, and anyone who can't abide by the rules can take the bus. It's not a punishment, just the consequence of not appreciating the privilege of getting a ride to school.

Now my time with the children is joyful and pleasant. I am able to see the beauty in the surrounding landscape and have pleasant conversations with them. I go to work and enjoy each employee, patient, and co-worker while feeling relaxed and not pressured.

I come home each night with enough time to do the things I want while interacting with my family in positive and meaningful ways. What a relief! We are no longer in constant conflict. When it is time to go to sleep, I fill my mind with pleasant thoughts and gratitude, and I quickly fall into restful sleep.

I am amazed at the transformation. It is as if I am on vacation every day.

This may sound like someone taking tranquilizers, but I am not. I can tell you my passion and enthusiasm are high, and I am actually getting more done, without any effort or stress.

More Gratitude

Whenever I hear myself start to complain or notice that someone else is trying to lead me there, I think about the many things I have to be thankful for. I get very specific, as there are so many things I used to take for granted. Walking down a hall, I am thankful for my ability to walk. I reel in my own graceful steps or play with my stride. I bless my sight and other senses and all of the pleasure they give me. My gratitude extends to the people who made my clothes, my car, the roads, and all things in this incredible world. Life is a joy of discovery as I keep noticing more things to be grateful for and appreciate.

If you are wondering what you have to be thankful for, just look around and imagine your life without anything you see or feel. Now notice what you have: your body parts, your abilities, your senses, your mind, your food, your clothes, your family, your friends....

> The great side effect of being grateful is that you feel wonderful and peaceful.

It takes a little effort at first because most of us find common ground with others by complaining together. When you start cultivating a positive frame of mind and seeing beauty everywhere, some of your complaining buddies may need to adjust. Be prepared to be considered a little crazy at first. Soon you will find that your friends may catch your "craziness" and enthusiasm.

Life is truly awe-inspiring. We just forget to notice.

Allow yourself to be awe-inspired. One way to encourage yourself is to keep a gratitude journal. Just think of 10 things that you are grateful for each day and write them in your journal. This is a great thing to do right before you go to sleep.

I, of course, don't keep a journal but do it out of habit mentally all day long. Even though a journal is a lovely concept, just saying it to yourself or writing it down on a piece of scrap paper or shouting it in your car with the windows up or down is also valid. Do it in the way that attracts you; "it" being the idea of being grateful continuously, which is really getting the BIG picture.

Prayers of Gratitude

Are there things in your life that you would like to change? Things that you would like to have? The most effective prayer is the prayer of gratitude. "Thank you for everything I already have." Say thank you as if you ALREADY have what you want.

If you say, "Please give me more money," what you are really saying is "I don't have enough." Instead, affirm that "I have enough. All the money I could possibly ever want is always here for me. I always have enough." Instead of concentrating on feelings about what you lack, develop the ability to feel what it feels like to have what you want already.

> *"Thank you, Divine within, for giving me everything I want. Thank you, Divine within, for giving me everything that I already have."*

Everything already exists in the universe. Your past and your future have already happened and are happening now! Your prayers can affirm this. The most positive prayer is "Thank you, God. Thank you for giving this to me. Thank you. I have this."

Imagine That You Already Have What You Want

The most powerful thing you can do is to imagine what you want, visualize it, and feel it. FEEL that you already have it; feel that you have everything that you want. If you want a job where people respect you, pretend that it exists right now. If you know it, it will be. When we understand this, we can begin to make conscious changes in our lives.

Take a moment to imagine that you are God or the Divine in your life. Now, here you are creating some entity or being to share eternity with. You have it all, anything you can imagine and more, anytime you want it. You have no insecurities or thoughts of inadequacy because you are God, for God's sake. If that is the case, then think about what kind of being you would create. You wouldn't create something that was less than you as it would get boring for eternity, or even just one lifetime for that matter. Personally, I would create something with the potential, at least, to be my equal. I would enjoy watching it learn and spread its wings. I would marvel at the least of its new feats and love it no matter what. I would comfort it when it needed it, and let it alone when it wanted to learn on its own. Does this sound familiar?

You were created in the image of God—the Creator—with the potential to be and do the same. Are you getting this? You have no limit but what you create for yourself.

My point right now, however, is that if you were the Divine, would you respond to whining or gratitude? Being grateful attracts more to be grateful for. Being ungrateful or complaining attracts more of the same. If I were the Divine and heard a complaint or request, I would probably realize that, if this being can't notice the trillions of gifts I had already given it, why would they notice the one more they are asking for? When we complain, we are actually saying I don't deserve it; I am a victim of circumstance.

I would probably give my creations anything they wanted no matter what unless they said "I don't want it, really." That is what we do when we judge ourselves or others. That is what we energetically say when we complain. That is what we do when we create hurdles to jump before we feel good about ourselves.

Gratitude is an ancient spiritual principle, and I have found that it works exquisitely in my own life. May you also live in beauty and gratitude. Realize that your divine heritage knows no limits, and inheritance implies that you don't really have to do anything to earn it but be born into it. Claim your inheritance by accepting it. Accept it by being grateful and knowing that you deserve it.

CHAPTER 5

Release Your Judgments

We are all naturally attracted to what makes us happy. What gets in the way of our natural happiness is the way we constantly judge ourselves and other people.

> Releasing judgment is not an altruistic thing to do; it's not even the "right" thing to do. It's the PRACTICAL thing to do.

Releasing judgment will give you your greatest joy and allow you to experience life to your fullest potential. Judgment works against your highest fulfillment, no matter what the judgment is about.

You judge people who don't work hard as "lazy," which in your judgment is an undesirable trait. *Then you wonder why you work so hard and never get to relax because there is so much to do.*

Someone calls you are a hard worker, and you feel good about yourself. You glow with your new label and feel *superior. Then you wonder why you never get a break and feel guilty for taking a vacation.*

In reality, we are all hard workers when we are motivated by passionate endeavors. Some of us have been blessed to be involved with activities we love. However, many of us work hard because we need external approval, so we push ourselves to get work done no matter how much it hurts us. We never approve of ourselves unless we are beating ourselves up with activity.

Even when we think we are open minded and nonjudgmental, there are layers of subconscious and subtle judgments that hold us back. It is part of peeling the onion of our true selves. As you journey into discovering what has been making your life tick and not exactly how you wanted it to tick, you will uncover and eliminate judgments.

When you eliminate judgments, you can then put all your creative energy into creating the life you were meant to live.

> We are all magnificent, and nothing that we do can add or take away from that.

"Teflon Woman" Tells All

When you know that you are valuable no matter what you do or don't do, life becomes an amazing experience. You can't know this about yourself unless you know this is true for everyone else as well. This is the truth of the TEFLON WOMAN—a name I was given when I was no longer affected by the negative comments of others. How do I do it? I don't take other people's judgments personally. They're not about me!

> I don't take anything personally.

I don't think badly of myself if someone says negative things about me, so I enjoy everybody I meet. I recommend that you think about going through life just enjoying everybody.

> There is no guilt when you make no one guilty.
> There is no obligation when you obligate no one.
> There are no mistakes when you make no one wrong.

The Rewards of Not Judging

The more you STOP judging people or events or things the less judgment weighs down on you and the freer you become. It is so liberating! The reason other people judge you is probably because you have an energy leak somewhere. If you really love yourself unconditionally, other people's judgments will just slide right off you—they have nowhere to stick. You too can be a Teflon Woman (or Man)! The only condition is that you must stop judging people (including yourself).

Not judging anything or anyone does not mean that you don't have strong and passionate preferences about what you want in life for yourself and others. You can and will have passionate preferences, but you will not spend any of your creative energy on the preferences of others. The preferences of others will only give you clarity about what you want or what you don't want. Then you can give your full creative attention to what you want.

You don't have to justify your preference by making other people's preferences wrong. That just keeps you from living your preference. You don't have to fight against anything you feel is wrong, for in giving it that attention, you are creating more of it. You don't have to feel negatively toward a criminal to have a preference for order and kind acts. In fact, sending judgmental negative feelings about those who commit acts that repel you only creates more of those very acts.

Dealing with Consequences

Of course, it is wise to choose your behaviors based on what the consequences will be. The consequences of running a red light are that you might harm someone or you might get a ticket. You can choose to avoid consequences without making a judgment that a particular action is good or bad, right or wrong.

What about Violence and Injustice?

There is a misconception that if everyone gave up all judgment of "right and wrong" that violence and injustice would prevail. When we look beyond these judgments, however, it is possible to see that people who are violent to others are in pain themselves. I am not excusing violent acts, but I know that judging people is not the answer. I want to END the cycle of violence. This requires not judging those who have been violent but rather recognizing the pain that caused the violence. This doesn't exclude removing violent people from society or facilitating constructive ways for them to make restitution.

Again, I make no judgment, and there are people who either are in so much pain they can't allow rehabilitation or we don't have a practical solution—yet.

People who have been hurt must also address the choice to be a victim. This does not excuse the behavior of abusers but allows the abused ones to have the opportunity to see a bigger picture and never be a victim again. We can even assist children who have been victimized and help them find the power to change their lives.

> I am talking about removing ALL judgments.

This means even getting rid of the judgment that BEING JUDGMENTAL is wrong! It's not wrong or bad. It's just not particularly useful. And the person who gets hurt by it the most is the one who is being judgmental. When you judge other people, there are a lot of things that YOU can't do because then you don't want to be as "bad" as them. When you judge other people, you are wasting your creative energy, so the life you want is further away. When you judge, you actually give your energy to the very thing you judge, so you make more of it.

How Your Own Judgments Hurt You

If you judge a man who is in great shape to be "self-centered" because he works out all the time and yet you want to be in great shape, you will not manifest a beautiful body. If you see a woman who seems to manifest a lot of free time and judge her to be "lazy" because she doesn't work as hard as you, then you will not manifest more free time. If you think a good mother ignores her own needs and thinks only of her children and judge the woman who takes time to pamper herself as "selfish," then you will not manifest time for yourself.

I am not making a judgment about right or wrong. I am not condoning any actions or condemning any. I am just trying to make you see that you are 100% responsible for all of what happens to you, no exceptions.

Jumping to Conclusions

Usually when we judge other people, we're just assuming information and jumping to conclusions with very little data. There is no way to really know the motivation behind other people's actions. We don't know all of their personal history, even if we think we do. We don't really know what the outcome of their choices will be either. We don't have a big enough picture to know how their thoughts and actions fit into the Divine plan. It's enough for each of us to figure out our own piece (and some of that is an eternal mystery too).

Recognizing Judgments

Blatant judgments are easy to recognize, but many judgments are less obvious and take some work to identify and eliminate. Sometimes it's hard to recognize judgments because they are woven into the very fiber of who you think you are. What, after all, makes someone a "good" child, mother, father, partner, worker, friend…and what constitutes a "bad" one?

Weeding Out Judgments

Like weeds, your judgments keep coming back unless you pull them out by the roots. Sometimes they masquerade as other plants, and you don't recognize them. Actually, if you want weeds and you're happy with them, great! However, if you want a rose garden, the weeds have to go.

Let's look at a few areas of judgment and see how they might affect you.

Judgments about Money

A lot of us have bought into the idea that "money is the root of all evil." For some of us, it is difficult to charge money or ask for money for services. It seems "selfish" to want it. Some judgmental concepts about money that many of us were taught contribute to this. For example, people with money are less "holy" or "not spiritual." They're "dishonest" and probably not "happy." If any of these judgments are operating in you, there is probably another judgment: Having a lot of money is "bad."

If someone has money, others may pour on even more judgments about them:

"Well, they just got lucky; they're not that talented."
"They have way more talent than I do."
"They have a degree that I don't have."
"They must know someone."
"Their parents had money, so they had an edge."
"They have a lot of money, but their personal lives are a wreck."

"I work just as hard as they do. Why should they get so much?"
"They work too hard; I don't want to do that."
"They have too much responsibility, and I don't want that kind of stress."
"They got in at the right time, and I missed the opportunity."

If you are thinking these kinds of things, you are creating a barrier to your own good fortune. You have difficulty having money because you expect it to be accompanied by poor health or personal disaster or hard work or talent. If you do happen to acquire money while you still carry these attitudes, you may become anxious that something will go wrong or that you will lose it. This is the world you create with judgmental thoughts about money.

Blessing the Flow of Money

Bless the money makers; bless the people who seem to get all the time off they want; bless the people who don't work as hard as you; bless all those who have what you want. Don't judge them—learn from them. When you can look at them without having to find fault, then you will no longer sabotage your own desires with jealousy and envy (obviously there may be qualities in these people you may or may not want to emulate, but don't judge).

> If you start to judge someone, try blessing them instead.

The next time you pay full price for something or get overcharged, bless the flow of money and the person that it benefits. Who's to say what the "right" or "fair" price is? It's all relative and changeable. (For example, salt used to be so precious it was used as money. Now it's thrown on streets to melt ice.) Make a habit of blessing people, and you will be too busy giving them your love to judge them.

Judgments about Success

"You have to do well in school to be successful." Now there's a judgment that doesn't hold water. I know lots of people who did well in school and are not happy and/or not financially successful. A CEO's grade point average is not what people talk about when they discuss her success. On the flip side, I know tons of people (that would be about 15 people per ton) who did not do well in school and overcame that stigma in order to succeed.

The most successful people just loved themselves, believed in themselves, and followed their passion, regardless of how well they did in school.

When you stop making judgments about what constitutes success (what jobs people have, how much money they have, where they live, what things they own, whether or not they have children …), you begin to recognize your freedom and enhance your ability to enjoy life. Bless the success of others, and you will be blessed.

Comparisons Are Judgments

You are in judgment every time you compare yourself to someone else. Here's a short list of common ways you might do this:

- If you hear another married couple is having more or less sex than you are, do you evaluate your relationship as better or worse than theirs? If someone gets flowers at work, do you feel jealous?
- If your children do not get good grades (a standard of comparison that doesn't necessarily measure their own unique forms of intelligence), do you push them to improve them?
- Do you compare your looks with others to keep score about who's in better shape, showing their age, etc.?
- Do you compare your home to other people's houses and feel inadequate?

When you stop defining yourself through comparison, you experience freedom from guilt, fear, worry, hurt, and insult. Comparisons are never accurate anyway and inevitably leave you feeling:

smug and superior (but limited because you have to uphold this status by NOT being the way you judge others) or

unhappy, bored, angry, tired, dissatisfied, and resentful. It is much more pleasant to enjoy who you are.

Because there is no other you, the logical conclusion is that you are the best you there is. Rejoice in that! The great news is, when you rejoice in yourself, you are then in a place to create an amazing life.

Labels

Labeling and defining ourselves and others by the roles we take on is a constant source of judgment. We take on roles (parent, doctor, laborer, lawyer, preacher, teacher, artist, wife, husband, mother-in-law, etc.) and then judge ourselves by how well we live up to these labels and definitions. A lucky few make up their own definitions. The unlucky ones abide by their family's or society's standards and definitions.

Each of us is a unique expression of the universe, and we cannot be defined in such limited ways. After all,

> Who we are a second ago is slightly different from who we are now.

Roles Isolate Us

Think about how roles separate us from one another. A physician may not feel that it's appropriate to show his/her vulnerability to patients or staff. This person has then eliminated any real contact with large groups of people and become isolated by conforming to the role called "doctor."

When you identify yourself with particular groups of people, you are then subject to all the rules, regulations, and self-limiting beliefs of that group. Every group has its advantages too. When you become aware of your roles and how others have defined them, you can choose to connect to only the advantages of the group and avoid the limitations.

The "Mother" Role

The cultural role of "mother" is a sticky one. On the one hand, you can get support from other mothers and a sense of belonging. You may also identify yourself with the wonderful things you do for your children. On the other hand, there is an unwritten societal rule for mothers that you must sacrifice yourself and always put your children first. You may continue living up to this image long after your children truly need you this way. As you accept yourself, you will confidently be a mother your own way and avoid this pitfall.

As your child grows, you will reclaim yourself knowing that this is also what is best for the child. On the other hand, if your true joy comes from mothering children, then you can create a lifetime of that in many ways. You just may not want to be attached to mothering your adult children the way you mothered them as toddlers. No one can judge what is right for you, but you will know that you are on the right path because you will be happy and those you are with will be happy as well.

Other Boxes

Many of us have learned to define ourselves not only by the roles we play but by what we say about our personal qualities. For example, **"I'm a stressed out person. It runs in my family."**

As a doctor, I'm very clear about the fallacy in the above statement.

> Stressed is a choice you make. It is not a personality trait, and there is no genetic predisposition for it.

You can learn to react to situations in a stressful way from your family, but no one is inherently a stressed-out person.

"I am not the expressive type" doesn't mean a person can't express themselves (we all can). It means that the person who says this has chosen not to be expressive because something painful from the past has left fear in this area. This person may not be conscious or aware of the fear and may not know how to go about being expressive, but by accepting the label, she or he eliminates the possibility of becoming expressive.

"I'm not talented. I'm disorganized. I'm ugly. I'm stupid. I'm not adventurous. I'm not the type who makes friends easily." Every negative and even positive way of defining yourself affects how you act and who you are in the world.

Again, I make no judgment, and if you are happy being inexpressive or stressed, then rejoice in that. In reality, we should be different with every person we connect with because each dynamic interaction is unique. You may be expressive with someone and quiet with another. You will know this effortlessly just by being in tune with who you are and loving that. When you are in that space, every single moment is full of adventure and mystery. You have the feeling that even your silence affects your destiny.

Beyond Labels and Judgments

Just as a child is protected from harm in his early years by rules, sometimes restrictions can serve a temporary purpose. The problem is that most of us become addicted to our restrictions, afraid to go outside the playpen. Healthy children will try to get out of their limitations as soon as they are able.

Many of us are still in the playpen, just becoming aware that there is a whole other exciting world out there once we get rid of our labels and judgments.

When you operate outside of judgment, it's easy to attract and create what you want.

We have difficult lives until we divest ourselves of our limiting beliefs, judgments, and fears. I guarantee that if you get rid of these limited ways of thinking, you will be magnetically attractive. Not only that, you will find the world filled with desirable people.

> The more you are true to yourself the more attractive you become.

Why? Because you are enthusiastic and happy about life and people find that very appealing. You find that you have no time to put other people down, and you are not threatened by anyone. You are confident because you are doing things that you love and are good at doing. You are uplifting to be around, and that is VERY appealing.

"I'm rich." "I'm a genius." "I'm in love." Start telling yourself that you are whatever you feel you want to be. If you tell yourself often enough, you will begin to believe it and so will everyone else around you. When you know it, it will become your reality.

Fear and Judgment

I want you to know that every fear you have is not real. And fear is the basis of all judging and disapproving attitudes.

> There is nothing to fear. In reality, the world is a safe and secure place. If you only knew how supportive it is, you would never fear anything.

When you throw away your fear, you begin to see the world as it really is. People will add to your life often with love and joy. You know how it feels to make someone happy, to give a gift they really want or help them when they least expect it? Imagine how it feels to other people when they get to do that for you! Learning to trust and allow the flow toward you is so much fun.

Would God make anything less than magnificent? You are part of that, and you deserve help in fulfilling your grand nature. Give yourself and others love, respect, and awed appreciation, and start to experience life as the God in physical expression that you are. *Everyone* is magnificent, and when two magnificent beings engage in a creative endeavor, there is even more magic.

It is arrogant to believe you must "be there" for everyone else and never accept help yourself.

Start asking for and accepting help, and you will get out of the isolated rat race that so many people live in. We live in an abundant world, and you have much to give as well. The universe was designed for cooperation.

The Library of Abundance

I went to a public library, and it was filled with books, computers with Internet access, videos, audio-cassettes, quiet places to study, and desks and tables to sit at. There were people there to help anyone use the equipment. It was like being in a candy store for the mind. I thought how incredible it is that anyone can come to this place to learn, study, develop ideas, gain information, or just have fun in a clean, comfortable space. We take this for granted, but the library is a wonderful institution and a symbol of what is available for all of us IF WE GO THERE.

Many of us sit in our fears and don't go to the library of Life. We judge ourselves as unworthy, so we don't even check out the resources available to us.

There are two major kinds of fear that limit us. The first fear is about survival: that we will die because we do not have basic things we need, such as food and shelter.

In an abundant world, do you think your basic needs would not be provided for? There are always resources available to you, but you must have the ability to NOTICE them. Fear can block your perception.

Imagine what it would be like not having anything at all: the heightened awareness you would have, the lack of responsibility, the adventure, the raw trust. Yes, I'm romanticizing it a bit, but with the right attitude, it can be this way.

The second fear is about status: that we will be embarrassed, humiliated, or seen as "less than" someone else.

This fear means you think your magnificence is dependent on someone else's opinion of you. You may think your value is defined by the things you own. You are not what you have. You are much greater than that.

Some of the most financially successful people have lost everything in their lives more than once and built up their wealth again. Two principles they have demonstrated over and over again are:

> When your idea of self is not attached to what you have, it is easier to attract more. Outer circumstances do not define you.

Releasing Expectations

So much of our anxiety is about how we live up to the expectations of others and how they live up to ours. All of these expectations are based on insecurities, fear, and the need to control others so we won't get more of what we don't want.

The ways we try to control each other actually hold our old fears and limitations in place.

When you let go of expectations and judgments (of yourself or others), you are no longer a slave to these types of anxieties, and you stop recreating what you don't want. Instead of ruminating about what your loved ones are doing wrong or not doing right, think about the things they do or just enjoy their loving presence for however long that is. You never know when they may not be with you again. Do you want to spend your moments with them cherishing the time or trying to change them?

Valuing Our Own Devices

"She was left to her own devices." Somehow, we have learned to hear this in a negative way. But what does it really mean? To me it means this person can create what she wants in her life and is not dependent on manipulating other people to get it.

How do you learn to trust your own ability to create what you want? First you must become aware of the "devices" you carry that belong to the past: parents, school, and society. Then get rid of the ones that no longer serve you.

> Start challenging every rule, every belief, every expectation, every obligation, and you will start to see that the majority of them are born of the need to control, which is a manifestation of fear.

Whether you are the one imposing these limited beliefs or someone else is, everyone involved in the interactions is fearful or the interaction would not occur.

Getting rid of your fears is the core of living a life that is heaven on earth, a life of unlimited freedom and potential, a life of manifesting all that you dreamed possible and then some.

Timing: A Lesson from the O.R.

I wasn't getting my cases done on time at the operating room (O.R.). I felt that the nurses were holding me up, and I was constantly anxious about this. I did not like the feeling of stress and pressure that was associated with pushing to get things done and being behind schedule.

I decided this had to change, so I started shifting my beliefs. I realized that I couldn't change how the operating room worked; it seemed no one could if you listened to the surgeons complaining. I decided that, no matter what, I would hold to the belief that ***everything happens for a reason.*** I stopped judging the nurses and the speed with which they did things. I decided to give positive thoughts to every person that I met. If I was delayed, I relaxed and read a book (this was a big improvement over pacing and feeling anxious or annoyed).

> I let go of my concept of how and when things had to happen.

When delays happened, I would say, "No problem, I'll just read my book. You take your time. Everything happens for a reason." The results were amazing. Now I am rarely delayed and usually it works out in my best interest if I am. Most likely I have another case scheduled in another room or something happens in the emergency room that I must attend to. It is uncanny the way it works.

Even better than that, I enjoy working with all the nurses now. I can honestly tell you every day is a joy because every single person is a joy to me. I enjoy every person, even people others find difficult to work with.

Life is wonderful since I gave up judging ANYONE.

CHAPTER 6

Meditate and Breathe

Want to lower your stress and enjoy your life more? I recommend you try meditation. This chapter covers this basic way of taking care of yourself.

Meditation helps you replenish your energy. Conscious breathing is the simplest and most accessible form of meditation that I have found. Here is some information to get you started (or encourage you to continue if you have already tried this).

There are many ways to meditate. Some are silent, some use sound, some use movement, and some use the breath as a way to focus your attention. You may be drawn to learn a particular method such as yoga, Tai Chi, transcendental meditation, or guided imagery. Maybe none of these appeal to you. That's okay; if meditation is right for you, you will find a way that works and is pleasurable.

You can live in a state of heaven on earth without ever formally meditating. If you are motivated to meditate, then do it. If not, then don't (that goes for anything I suggest or that you get from any other book, CD, or course). The best meditation technique for you may be one you create yourself. Meanwhile, experiment and be patient with yourself.

What Is Meditation?

I define meditation as taking time to connect with God and your divine self. You can meditate once a day, in several blocks of time throughout your day, or continuously in every moment. Your entire day can be a meditation. (This is my personal choice.)

You actually enter a meditative state when you are in the zone. In fact, have you ever driven somewhere and got there without remembering the drive, lost in thought and working on automatic, or missed your exit? That may have been a meditative state.

Scientifically, meditation is a state of relaxation while you are still alert, and the brain waves are alpha brain waves sometimes dipping into theta brain waves. It has been shown that doing some form of meditation on a regular basis increases health, longevity, and youthfulness.

The real benefit, in my humble opinion, is the reconnection of you with your divine self or God and, of course, the incredible pleasure of it.

Getting Past Resistance to Meditation

Getting quiet and looking within can be a scary prospect. There is a good reason why some people talk about doing it, tell others to do it, and expound on the value and benefit in doing it but never get around to it themselves.

Instructions about the nuts and bolts of meditation are sometimes complicated and shrouded in ritual and mystery. It's really a simple thing to do. Relax, let go, and be patient.

> Meditation is a natural state of being.

What if you were kept from walking for the first 20 years of your life? You might be afraid to try it. What if someone then told you that walking was your natural way of moving? Once you realized this was the truth, you would learn to walk quite naturally, probably without instruction. There is a direct parallel with meditation.

Instruction Is Useful for Some People

For some people, instruction in meditation is a good way to get started. There are many excellent classes, teachers, CDs, etc., to help you orient yourself. Whatever you choose, I recommend that you remember that any instruction or guidance is just that! You are the one who knows what is right for you. Look within. Find out who you are. Trust your intuition, and develop your own relationship with the Divine. You will know you are on the right path because it will feel good to you, and it will be easy.

How I Started Meditating

There was a shortage of surgeons at my hospital. One surgeon was ill, and one was pregnant, so we were operating with half of our usual staff. We were all very stressed out. I had heard that meditation might help me relax.

I tried to meditate on my own, but I wasn't really getting it, so I took a transcendental meditation course. I learned that you can't do it wrong! I learned it's just a matter of sitting down, relaxing, and focusing. (They also taught me a sound to focus on, but I believe that it is optional.) I started meditating regularly, and it really helped me handle my work and my life more peacefully.

Around that same time there was one week where I was the only general surgeon for the entire week because the other surgeon was away due to a death in his family. What would have been impossible and full of stress was relaxed and easy. I was amazed that I could handle the week without stress and used meditation whenever I had a few minutes anytime I could find a chair in a quiet area.

I did get instruction through the TM course and also read about it and listened to many CDs about meditation in other forms. Hopefully, I can give you the quick and easy synopsis.

Finding Time to Meditate

Teachers of transcendental meditation recommend that you meditate as soon as you wake up in the morning and at about 6:00 in the evening. The first period of meditation helps you focus yourself for the day, and the second helps you rejuvenate yourself for the evening. They say that if you fall asleep during meditation, it means you need the sleep! There is nothing wrong with falling asleep.

After I had my son, I stopped sitting down for 20 minutes twice a day as I was originally instructed to do. Now I do shorter meditations throughout the day. Even a minute or two helps. Whenever I get a chance, I sit down and meditate. When I can't sit down, I pause in what I'm doing and take a few deep breaths.

Positive Effects of Meditation

For me, the effects of meditation have been quite significant. I find that I am always relaxed now. I feel less stressed. I feel like I live in a state of constant prayer and connection to God. Time seems more expansive, and I actually get more things done in a minimal amount of time.

In fact, I have been hooked up to biofeedback machines and have been found to be able to reach the alpha wave state in the brain almost immediately. This state is associated with the meditation state and responsible for many health benefits. This is when you are in an alert, relaxed state of mind. If I can do it anytime, you can too. We all do it unconsciously every day but can make a conscious choice to do it more often.

Meditating for Insight

Meditation is not just about relaxation. It is also an opportunity to gain insight. Sometimes new clarity will come to you during the time you are meditating, but often it comes afterwards. You may find that you are clearer about where you want to go with your life and what you are doing or not doing. You start to trust your instincts a little bit more. Miracles (even little ones such as easily finding parking spaces) begin to happen more frequently. Your day seems to flow instead of being a struggle.

Breathing Is the Simplest Technique

I find the simplest technique is just concentrating on the breath. It is useful to sit down to do this, but you can actually meditate in any position: sitting, lying down, or standing up. Sitting meditation is a really nice, relaxing thing to do; it can be done most places and is more conducive to staying alert while relaxed.

Once you have found a comfortable position, start counting down slowly with each breath from ten to one. You may never get to one because you will start thinking about other things. When this happens, you just acknowledge it, realize that you are thinking, and then bring your awareness back to the breath. Don't be concerned about the thought or that you were thinking at all; just let it pass and go back to the counting from the beginning at ten so you don't have to "think" about where you were. You may never get to one, but who's counting? It doesn't matter.

Deep Breathing

In the tradition of Chinese medicine, there is an exercise that involves just taking deep breaths throughout the day. Whenever the idea occurs to you, take a series of one to ten deep breaths or just focus on an aspect of the breathing cycle. Even if you do it a couple of times a day, you will experience a significant change in your life. I stop and take three deep breaths whenever I feel like I am getting stressed, sick, or pressured. I also do it when I want to send a blessing or have a pleasurable thought or moment. It really calms me down and helps me think more clearly no matter what the circumstances.

Allow yourself to take frequent deep breaths. You can't be stressed when you are focusing on taking a deep breath. When you remember to breathe, you remember who you truly are—a magnificent, spiritual being, who is here in this body for a brief moment but eternal.

Medical Effects of Meditation

The meditative state is called the Relaxation Response in medicine. It lowers your cholesterol, blood pressure, and heart rate, and it helps you think more clearly. Scientists found in one study that people who mediate regularly look younger, live longer, and see doctors 85% less than people who don't. That is significant!

I have enjoyed life so much more since I started meditating and just letting things go. I recommend that you also learn to let things go.

There Is Nothing You Have to Do

I used to have lists of things I thought I needed to do. Now I rarely make lists unless I am inspired to do so. Even so, lists are not good or bad but can be used as a crutch or distraction if they rule you. They can also be used as a tool of inspiration. I have found I don't need lists to keep me on track. I just pay attention in the moment, and the people making lists around me keep me posted. You too will find your natural rhythm as you just breathe and pay attention. In reality, the activities you are truly passionate about will not be forgotten.

There are no rules on how to live your life. When you find your purpose, you will do it all naturally. Anything that requires struggle is only a struggle because you created it that way or you aren't following your truth. That goes for meditation as well, so don't add it to your "list" of things to do if it doesn't attract you.

More Ways to Use Your Breath

Here are some methods of breath work you can incorporate into your everyday life. You can do this at any time you have a moment. Conscious breathing will relax you and energize you when you need it.

1. Pay attention to your breath while you are waiting for an elevator or for traffic to move or while you are standing in line.
2. Every time you think about it, focus on an aspect of the act of breathing. For example:
   ‣ the rise and fall of your chest
   ‣ the sound of your breath
   ‣ feeling of the flow of air through your nostrils
3. Use your breath to transform negative emotions and relax in the midst of stressful situations. Focus on your breath:
   ‣ when you are feeling annoyed or angry.
   ‣ when your mind takes you on a guilt trip or worry fantasy.
   ‣ when someone finds fault with you.
   ‣ when you are feeling overwhelmed or pressured.
   ‣ whenever you have any feeling you don't want to have.

Conscious breathing takes no time from your day and requires no money. It will make an incredible difference in your life.

Meditating with Sound

Wayne Dyer teaches a Chinese tradition of meditation based on sound. You use the sound "ah" in the morning because that is for opening up. Just open your mouth and let the "ah" sound come out. You keep doing that until the sound gets quieter and quieter, and then it becomes an internal "ah." At night, you use the sound "ohm" because that is for quieting and closure.

Meditating with "ah" and "ohm" is called Manifesting Meditation. It is said that if you do it regularly, you will be able to manifest, attract, and create what you want in your life.

Other Ways to Meditate

Another way to meditate is a walking meditation where you walk a circular path or back in forth path and just focus on each step you take. This is a good way for someone who feels they just can't sit still until they find they can sit still.

One of my favorite ways to meditate is to listen to CDs from Holosync TM, where there are sounds embedded in the CDs that stimulate the alpha wave state. It seems like a great way to meditate without having to "learn" how. The CDs are very relaxing and can be found at www.centerpointe.com.

Living in the Zone

Some people enter a relaxed, meditative state when they run or dance. They call it being in the "zone" when the mind is relaxed and alert and everything one does seems effortless. This is a natural meditation and can be achieved during many activities, especially repetitive ones.

I often experience being in the zone when I perform surgery. I find myself in a meditative state where I am focused and peaceful, and this ability to be in the zone or enter a peaceful state is available to all of us all the time.

CHAPTER 7

Imagine Your World into Reality

The average person thinks about 60,000 thoughts a day. Every one of them is creating your universe and the world you experience each moment. You might as well use them positively to create what you want!

You can have miraculous changes in your life if you change your thoughts.

> *"Change your thoughts, change your life."*
> — Dr. Wayne Dyer

Change your beliefs, and your reality will change. I can't tell you how it happens, but it truly does. People actually change. Some people get better looking. Some people get more graceful. Some people start doing things you might think they could never do in a million years. I challenge you to change your thinking and test this out in your own life. Start by consciously talking to yourself.

> "As you believe, so it will be done to you."
> — Jesus Christ

How to Talk to Yourself

Tell yourself how great you are, how much fun you are to be with, and how attractive you are. For the sake of this exercise, try this out loud. "You are so much fun to be with, and you are so attractive!"

If you make a "mistake" by doing something you wish you hadn't or failing to do something you think you should have, tell yourself it was meant to be and will work out for the best in the end. Whatever happens is meant to happen.

Catch yourself as soon as you start berating or judging yourself, and give yourself permission to be perfectly flawed.

Appreciate Other People

Purposely think positive thoughts about every person you see, even strangers on the street.

This will train your renegade mind to focus on what is good about each person you notice. You can start with superficial things, such as hairstyles or jeweler or clothing. Notice things you like about the way someone walks or talks. It really doesn't matter what you appreciate or if you say it out loud. It only matters that it is a pleasant thought for you, positive toward the other person, and genuine. You truly can find something genuinely positive about every person you encounter. I challenge you to make it a habit.

This exercise undoes the tendency we all have to make comparisons and tear down another person in order to think more highly of ourselves OR to tear down ourselves in the comparison because we've been taught we aren't that good.

Retraining your mind to think good thoughts about other people will stop you from thinking negative thoughts about yourself. Comparing ourselves to each other is so deeply entrenched in us that we often do it without conscious thought. This wastes a lot of energy!

Consciously thinking positive thoughts about yourself and others releases your infinite supply of energy and love from within.

Use Your Imagination

You can use your imagination to envision how you want things to be in the near and far future. Imagine yourself as someone who stirs in you the feeling of being magnificent, respected, adored, and secure. I occasionally pretend I am a Greek goddess or a top runway model. I pretend people are turning to watch me, wondering if I am who they think I am, noticing my air of confidence and beauty. Sometimes while I'm driving my Suburban, I pretend I'm in a Jaguar and admire the luxurious interior and smooth ride. Sometimes I imagine I am a small child and wonder at the simple, small things I see, like an elevator button or a beautiful flower.

Now, if you can really feel as if your imagined state is real and enjoy that feeling, you are on your way to manifesting a life that gives you "real" reasons to feel that way.

Create Something out of Nothing

If you really think about it, just lifting an arm is creating something out of nothing. The mind is not located in the brain. The mind is nonlocal and undefined. This definition sounds like the Divine, doesn't it? You think a thought to lift your arm, and that non-local, non-physical thought causes the brain to be stimulated to move your arm through the appropriate pathways in the physical world. Life is truly nothing short of a miracle.

In every circumstance, you are choosing the thoughts you have on purpose or by default. Your thoughts are creating the feelings you have, and that is what life is all about. Your thoughts create the reality that you experience, the "when and how" of events that happen, the people who are drawn into your life, the amount of money you have, and even the quantity of life you live.

Turn Your Worries and Your Guilt Around

If you have a worry, take the worried thought and turn it around. Change it into a thought about what you WANT. Worried about being late for an appointment? Imagine yourself arriving at JUST THE RIGHT MOMENT.

If you have a guilty thought, tell yourself that all that has happened was meant to be and could not have been different. Do you feel bad that you lost an important document? Tell yourself there's a reason for it that improves the situation (even if you can't see what it is yet).

Affirmations and Prayers

Some people call these intentional positive thoughts affirmations. Others call them prayers. In studies of intentional thoughts such as these, the most effective ones are stated in the present tense without negative words such as "not" or "no."

State what you want to happen. Do not state what you do not want to happen. Looking for a new job? "Thank you for this great job! I enjoy using my talents and making more money." Do not state, "I don't want to work at the job I have where I don't make enough money."

State your desire as if what you want exists right now, and give thanks for it in the present.

Imagine a picture of what you want to manifest and evoke the feeling of having it already. Consciously use your imagination as often as possible, and you will build up your imaging "muscles" to create what you want.

All-Purpose Affirmations

> I am love, I am light.

This was the first affirmation I started playing with. I used it whenever I felt sad or mad or envious. Then I kept adding concepts I wanted to incorporate into my life. This is my current all-purpose affirmation:

> I am love, I am light, I am peace, I am health, I am beauty, I am passion, I am power, I am abundant.

If I feel a cold coming on, I can stop it dead in its tracks by using my all-purpose affirmation! This is how I show myself, on an ongoing basis, that anything is possible.

You are welcome to use my affirmation or come up one of your own that is equally brilliant (you know the things you need to affirm for yourself, and you can keep revising it as you go the way I did).

Affirmations for Parents

If you are a parent, you probably feel upset about your children now and then. (How's that for an understatement?) These are two affirmations that have helped me to stop parenting with guilt and worry. I suggest you use these affirmations or make up your own.

1. My children are always safe and happy, protected from all physical and emotional harm.
2. My children are talented and succeed in all aspects of their lives.

The best thing you can do for your children is to model living a balanced, passionate, and happy life. They will find their way to success quicker with an example like that. Release yourself from anger, worry, and guilt and know that your child is safe and talented enough to be self-motivated to succeed in the areas of his or her own interest. By knowing this, you free your child to be creative where she or he wants and not waste energy by doing things through obligation instead of passion. When you free yourself and lead by example, your precious child does not have to follow you into your old prison.

How I Stopped Worrying about My Son

I am divorced from the father of my first son. Our arrangement is that my son spends three out of four weekends with his father. I used to feel terrible guilt and worry when my son was gone, even though, rationally, I knew he was safe and having a good time (his father really is an excellent father, and they like to go roller-blading, visit museums, and play baseball—stuff that I really don't enjoy).

But I missed my son, and I worried about him. Instead of wallowing in that, I started consciously sending out positive affirmations about him. I would say, "My son enjoys his time with his father and needs it. He is safe and happy and well balanced."

I also recognized my own guilt about being divorced and a working mother played into my worry. Often they go hand in hand, so I used the affirmation: "My son knows he is unconditionally loved by me and has as much interaction with me as he wants."

This worked! I don't worry about my son anymore. I don't sit and pine for my son or feel guilty, but I get on with my life and enjoy it. I know I have contributed to my son's great relationship with his father, and they have a lot of fun together. I know he is happy and able to create the life that he wants.

Medical Effects of Positive Thinking

When you change how you think, you change how you feel. Scientific literature now documents that joy, happiness, and inspiration stimulate your immune system. There was a study done about 20 years ago that rated people on their ability to experience pleasure. Those that scored lowest had a 10% survival rate in 20 years, and those that scored highest had a 90% survival rate in that same time period! (The American Holistic Health Association's Complete Guide to Alternative Medicine) Having pleasure in your life actually makes you healthier.

Creating Your Own Reality

You create your own reality with thought and intention. I was able to embrace this concept as I saw it demonstrated in my own life. I began experimenting with changing my thoughts and beliefs with the sole intention of changing myself, making myself feel better, and finding ways to handle a few difficult circumstances. It turned out that, when I changed, my whole world changed. Other people changed around me, or they left. I have proof now that my world is a reflection of my beliefs. I am challenging you to discover this for yourself.

Our Thoughts Affect the Physical World

Physicists are finding that all things are connected throughout the universe. Deepak Chopra has been instrumental in bringing these concepts to my attention and explaining things in eye-opening ways for me. I would recommend his books to the novice who has no knowledge of physics, and then you can study more deeply if you are interested. Of great significance is the fact that science proves that at any given moment we all have in our own body one million atoms that also existed in any given being, including Christ, Buddha, and anyone else you admire. We give a lot of power to physical connection but fail to realize that we are truly physically connected to all things as the atoms that make us up change completely every two years (some are recycled even faster).

In addition, what makes the physical world physical is an illusion. We are all made up of atoms that are 99.999% space, and the rest of it is energy leaping in and out of our ability to experience it. Let that sink in, and you will begin to see things from a different perspective.

I asked my son what the meaning of life was on one of our journeys to school in the morning, hoping to stir in him some philosophical wanderings. His answer was profound in his teenager state of being. He said, "Whatever," and the truth is the meaning of life is whatever you give it, nothing more or less.

The Placebo Effect

I think all the healing modalities work because we make them work. This includes conventional medicine and drugs as well as alternative remedies. We make them work!

In one drug test, scientists gave the taste and smell of a particular drug to half of the experimental subjects and an actual dosage to the other half. The first group had the same physical reaction as if they had been given the actual drug. They were cured even though they did not ingest any of the substance! They just thought it worked, and it did.

This is called the placebo effect, when healing happens because people believe they are taking a drug even though they're not (often this is done with pills that look the same as "the real thing" but aren't). In some studies, the rate of cure is as high as 70%. People are healed by the *thought* that they are taking something effective, not by the actual substance.

When people come to see me as a doctor, it is not just the medicine I give them that cures them. Healing comes from our interaction and from their trust and belief in me.

There are some people who don't believe in anything, and I cannot cure them because they do not want to be cured. A physician just can't help them. It is truly an art to be a doctor. I think many physicians are getting back to this understanding. In medical school, doctors have been taught to see patients as just diseased parts in need of healing. Now doctors are coming back to the understanding that all of a patient's systems are interconnected.

You Make Things Happen with Your Thoughts

When you think your thoughts, you make things happen, both consciously and unconsciously. Think about the significance of this! It's huge. Think about people in love or parents loving their children. Think about the support provided by their thoughts. When you realize what kind of an effect you can have, it becomes important to choose what you want to believe. If you believe it can happen, it will happen. You are in charge, and you make it so.

The World Is an Illusion

Start by thinking that this world is an illusion—one that you have created. Everything you experience has passed through your mind already—everything. For example, everything you see had to come from a light source, go through your eye to your optic nerve, and be processed by your brain, and then you "saw" it. When you look in the mirror, you are not seeing yourself. You are seeing the brain's interpretation of a light reflection. Begin to entertain the possibility that everybody sees differently because they receive and interpret the light reflections that come to them differently.

There may be some people who find you extremely attractive and other people who find you extremely unattractive, or some people who think you are absurd and then others who think you are telling the truth. You can't really go by anybody else's interpretation because they all see life differently.

Every atom that makes up this entire world is 99.999% space. That means we are predominately space, and yet I feel solid to myself. That is my perception. It is actually not objective reality; that is what I choose to make my reality. It is an illusion, and who knows what other illusions make up our belief systems.

You can't see electricity, right? But you believe in it, and you use it. You can't see the radio waves in this room, but when you turn the radio on, you hear the songs, so they are there, correct? In fact, there are thousands of stations playing right in the room you occupy, and you can't hear them because you do not have the receptors to hear them all at once. But they exist, and they are there. So it is a matter of what receptors we have. Other people may have receptors that we don't and may interpret data from their senses very differently than you or me. We may wonder why that good looking woman is with that odd looking guy. "I don't know what she sees in him."

The Strongest Thought Wins

Make your own decisions about who you are, and in most instances, everybody else follows your opinion because the strongest thought wins. If you have a strong opinion about yourself, almost everybody will start believing that opinion. If you are kind of wishy-washy, you are going to take on everybody else's opinions. Then you find that some days you inexplicably feel really good, and some days you feel really bad. And some days you feel really on top of things, and some days you don't. I used to think that was the roller coaster of life and just part of my hormonal fluctuations. It doesn't have to be that way.

> You do not have to have emotional ups and downs. You don't have to be a victim to your feelings (unless you want to be).

Before I "got" this concept, I would periodically wallow in self-pity. I would feel sad or withdrawn all day long over small things, and they are all small things when you really get down to it. I got over it when I realized I had given up my own choice of how I wanted to feel.

Let Your Feelings Out

I'm not suggesting that you fake your feelings. You have to admit and honor your anger if you are angry. Recognize it. Feel it. Realize it. If you try to fake it by being laid back, you are holding all that anger inside of you. This just stresses and suppresses your immune system. Any unexpressed emotion is going to suppress your immune system.

Expressing and honoring an emotion is not the same as letting it control you or your behavior. In fact, you don't have to discuss it with the person you feel is responsible because, when you get right down to it, only you are responsible for your emotions. On the other hand, you have to admit that you are choosing the emotion and deal with the choice not cover it up and pretend that you didn't choose it.

Even expressing intense sadness will actually enhance your immune system.

You have to let that stuff out. I still cry regularly, but now it is usually a cry of joy or intense gratitude and love. I may experience a deep feeling of love or hear a song, and it will just thrill me. Or I will look at my son while he is sleeping, and tears of love will come to my eyes. When you begin to realize that you can actually affect the world with your positive thinking, you become deeply inspired and feel intense emotions on a daily basis.

Unexpected Gifts

You learn to frame everything in positive terms. When things happen that you didn't plan, or events don't go the way you wanted them to go, you believe that it had to happen that way and wonder what you can get out of it. You are always going to get something better out of something that seems bad. Every time you lose something, something better is going to come to you. All you have to do is open your eyes. Instead of thinking, "What did I do to deserve this?" you say, "Thank you," and open your eyes to the gift that you are being given.

Get Fired

My sister lost her job at a company where she had worked for 10 years. Her superiors said she wasn't working up to her potential. According to her, they were not supportive and sometimes downright nasty. She definitely wanted to work for supportive people and felt she deserved to be making more than she was making. Finally, she got fired. At first she was devastated, but as I reminded her that all clouds have their silver lining, she calmed down.

Within a week, she had a better job with people who supported her, and she started making much more money. Everything is happening exactly the way it is supposed to. Although everything does not go our way at first, it is just God giving us something better or giving us a little guidance or a little push. Sometimes you ask for that push to the next level when you say something like, "I hate my job." All of a sudden you get fired, and you think, "What happened?" Well, you asked for a better job. You just got fired, and now you are available for a better job!

Whatever happens, on some level, you have asked for it. Open your eyes and see what you asked for.

Did you know that our prayers are always answered? I know mine are. Sometimes I am surprised at what I was asking for. You get what you ask for! Most of us go around not realizing what we are asking for and how we are asking for it.

All your thoughts add up. You may think, "May I please have this car?" But at the same time, you may also be worrying about money, saying to yourself, "I just don't have enough." In this case, your thoughts are mixed together and cancelling each other out!

Use your thoughts wisely, and realize they are an incredibly powerful force. You CAN use them to change the world and yourself.

Start thinking that you have enough. Realize that you do have everything you want. What you put out there with your thoughts is going to come back to you. Be careful—if you are putting out that you are lacking something, that you're not pretty, that you're not deserving, etc., these are the things you are going to get back.

Undoing Worry

I stopped worrying by substituting anxious thoughts with positive affirmations. You can do that with any worrying thought too. Just take that worrying thought and say, "Oops! That is a worrying thought." Write it down. Next, think a positive thought that relates to the same topic. Say this positive affirmation over and over again until the worrying thought is gone.

You can't tell your mind not to do something, but you can tell it to do something else. Give it something else to think instead of what you don't want to think.

Create your life consciously. Obsess over positive thoughts, and eventually you will believe them, and they will become the truth. That is what I did, and now it IS the truth in my world. I don't ask you to believe what I am saying, but what do you have to lose in trying to think differently? The proof will be in your experience.

Imagine You Have Special Powers

Imagine how your life would be different if you had special powers. You could heal people by looking at them, touching them, or just thinking about them. You could heal people by smiling at them. You could make their lives better. You could change things in the world just by thinking.

Imagine you have that power. How would life be different? Would you walk through life a little bit differently? Would you meet your destiny a little bit more confidently? Would you let the mundane things be less important, and would you always have your eyes open for chances to heal somebody? I think so.

I think every person truly wants to be a healer and do things that uplift and help others. I see that in everyone I know and meet. I find that people are truly good and that they only hurt others when they too are in pain. That is my reality.

By the way, you do have those powers. If you stop focusing your energy on the few things in your life that are not going the way you want and start focusing on the things that work well, you will cause universal changes and healing.

Create Wild Excuses/Give Others the Benefit of the Doubt

When things don't go your way, or someone in your life falls short of your mark, or a co-worker doesn't come through, you can use your imagination to create a wild excuse that gives them more than the benefit of the doubt. Not only will you strengthen your powers of imagination, it will reduce your anger. It doesn't help you to be angry about something you have no control over. This doesn't mean that you have to accept behavior that doesn't serve you, but it does keep you in a positive frame of mind, which leads to clearer and more productive decisions and solutions.

For example, someone shows up late for a meeting. You make up some incredible excuse for them and are upbeat for the meeting. "He had to wrestle a shark out of his neighbor's water tank." You don't have to give energy to whether you are going to believe his excuse because you already have one to use.

If this becomes a pattern in your dealings with this person, it doesn't matter what their excuse is anyway. If they are attracting valid circumstances into their life that cause them to be late for meetings, then that is as much a problem as if they are purposely late or have no valid excuse. It has the same effect on your life regardless of the reason.

You must decide whether this person is worth the wait or not. There is no need for emotional turmoil on your part. If you decide they are worth waiting for, then you prepare for the wait with a book, some work, or some meditation. If you decide they are not worth the wait, or you don't have time for waiting, then you stop meeting with that person.

You may find that once you are no longer bothered by someone being late, the person may stop being late. This has often been my experience. Obviously, if this is an important relationship that you can't terminate, with a co-worker or family member, go back to plan A. Take a book or use the time to meditate. Know that you have attracted this into your life, and when you find the reason why, it will stop. Know also that everything happens for a reason. If you are late for your next appointment because of another person's tardiness, most likely the person you are late for is struggling with the same issues you are.

Giving people the benefit of the doubt is a great way to shape the world into a place where you are surrounded by supportive and loving people. Using your imagination to create scenarios that excuse people for falling short of your expectations takes the animosity out of the moment.

Remember to take full responsibility for everything that happens. To live this way gives you peace in every moment without anger or blame. Surprisingly, it actually eliminates the issue in your life magically. Time and time again when I stopped being bothered by something or giving it any negative emotional response, those events stopped occurring in my life. It was a pleasant surprise for me, and now I know it to be the truth.

Be Playful

If you observe children playing fantasy games, you will notice that they really become what they pretend and feel all the feelings. I invite you to reclaim this kind of playful pretending. Imagine your life is everything you dreamed it could be. Imagine that you have never before experienced something you do every day, and look at it through the eyes of someone from a distant planet or 200 years ago. When you play with life, you have more fun AND actively create your dreams. Be like children. The joy you can regain is immeasurable.

I like to go to the mall with my sunglasses on and pretend that I am a super model incognito. I like to imagine what it would feel like to be in great shape and have people looking my way with admiration, wondering who I am. I imagine that I make millions and can buy whatever I want. Now, that is a fantastic feeling! It makes the chore of going to a mall so much more pleasurable. The more you engage in using your imagination, the easier it becomes.

I fully hope to be able to write about how I am in better shape and making millions in my next book. Although, I have to say, I am going in that direction on all counts already.

Create Adventures

Imagine that there is a message in every little thing that happens and every person you meet. There actually is, but if you don't believe it, just pretend this for a while. This requires that you be present in the moment like a detective or spy so you don't miss any clues. Who knows? The bum on the street may be your contact or a master disguised to teach you your next lesson.

Instead of grinding your teeth in traffic, pretend that had you not been stuck in traffic you would have been killed in an accident. That puts a whole new spin on the situation.

Imagine that you can give people whatever they want as anonymous gifts. You can send a new car to all your children, pay off their loans, and fund a huge family cruise without anyone knowing it was you.

There have been studies* that show you affect the immune system of the people around you when you meditate. You may want to imagine that being in a peaceful state stimulates the immune system of the people you are with. In that case, you are a healer walking the streets of your town. Doesn't that make you feel different about who you are or what you are doing?

Your Invitation

I invite you to test out the idea that "thought creates reality." For me, this is the only plausible explanation for how the world works. I think you will see amazing results if you try

---

* Kuchinskas, Susan. "Meditation Heals Body and Mind." WebMD the Magazine - Feature. < http://www.webmd.com/mental-health/features/meditation-heals-body-and-mind>

this path of imagination for a few months. It takes no money and requires no major life changes or physical effort. The only requirements for this experiment are that you change how you think and assume total responsibility for your life without blaming yourself or others.

Your thoughts are the creative force of the world.

Maybe you have thought that the world just began from nothing or maybe that God created the world and finished it all at once. Creation is an ongoing process!

You are the physical manifestation of God, the creative force, divine intelligence, the other side of nothing, on this earth. Every thought you think has an effect on the world. The power behind this concept is breathtaking. Whenever you have a positive thought, you are making the whole world a better place as well as improving your immediate world. When you have a negative thought, you are taking the world down a peg. When you put your trust or power or belief in a group of people or a concept, your creative force is added to theirs. If you have the mistaken idea that you are insignificant, then think again. The sum total of all human beliefs and thoughts create the world we live in, and your personal beliefs and thoughts create your own life.

The Payoff

When you spend your time using your mind in a positive and imaginative way, it prevents you from having negative thoughts and ruminating over worry and guilt. After a while, this way of thinking becomes second nature. You start seeing concrete proof that the world is a reflection of what you think, and life becomes fluid, easy, and joyful. You get to a point where your peace and joy are constant. You can't be offended or hurt. You have only patience and love for yourself and, therefore, all others. Your whole life will feel like you are on vacation surrounded by all of your favorite people. You will be excited about each day. You won't be waiting for anything in the future because you are having so much fun in the present.

So I invite you to join me in a life of delight! What a great experiment this is.

Conclusion

I know that if I can turn a life of struggle into peace and joy and miraculous events without effort, so can you. I know that it will be the easiest thing you ever had to do because it involves a change in the habit of your thoughts and nothing else.

Choose your joy!

Even if you don't think you are the orchestrator of your life, entertain the possibility that you are, and start choosing differently. Question all things and all beliefs that have led you to the life you live. In every moment, find a way to think about the circumstance you are experiencing in a way that makes you feel better if not great. Allow yourself to have the feelings you want independent of the circumstances, and the circumstances will change to match your feelings.

Listen to your inner voice!

Only listen to the true inner voice, and that voice will always support you and love you and cherish you. Ignore any other voices in your head. Ignore the one that says you are not worthy or adequate or lovable. Your true self is magnificent and spectacular. Your true self is unlimited and capable of making all your dreams come true without effort. Your true inner voice will support and reinforce that reality. Any time the voice inside your head makes you feel less than magnificent, turn it off and listen for the truth, which is that you are magnificent and unlimited and deserving of all that you want without struggle.

Take back your power!

There is no one on this earth who knows what is best for you but you. There is no one else on this earth who is better than you at figuring out what is right for you. Relearn how to make your own decisions and follow your passion and pleasure. You were born with specific desires and interests that are unique to only you. You chose them to be your guide to your greatest experience, so follow your own inner guidance. You will live the life you dream of having and help everyone around you live their own. Be selfish for the greater good of all.

Live in beauty and gratitude!

The quickest way to being in the most creative and supportive energy is to be appreciative of all that you are and live. The great thing about this life is that every moment there is an infinite number of things to appreciate. Get in the habit of appreciating what is to get to what is next. When you train yourself to think a good thought about each person you meet, not only do you change the world for good, but you become a person of influence.

Release your judgments!

Each time you judge another or yourself, you keep yourself from all that you want to have and be in your life. You can have strong preferences. In fact, you were born to have them. It is the judging of any child of the universe to be less than magnificent that stops the flow of good things. Whether you judge yourself or another, it will make your life less wonderful and more difficult. The world is designed to make it possible for all to have exactly what they want provided they put their attention on what they want. You can't have your attention on judging another and keep it on what you want. It is impossible.

Meditate and breathe!

There are so many ways to take your mind to a place that relaxes you. If all else fails, just giving yourself permission to stop the chatter of the habits of your thoughts will help you retrain your mind to go where you want it to go. Guided imagery, self-hypnosis, meditation, or breathing exercises done regularly will help you gain control of your powerful mind. Once you are in control, then all things are possible.

Imagine your world into reality!

Lastly, exercise your right to create spectacular experiences. Reclaim your ability to imagine yourself into the scene you desire, and when it feels good to imagine the event, the event is soon to be a reality. There is no downside to this exercise, and you will see the results in real life and know how incredibly powerful you are.

Enjoy your life the way you intended to enjoy it.

References

Alexander, Thea. *2150AD*. Time Warner Publishing M/M, 1989.

Altea, Rosemary. *The Eagle and the Rose: A Remarkable True Story.* Grand Central Publishing, 2001.

Altea, Rosemary. *You Own the Power: Stories and Exercises to Inspire and Unleash the Force Within.* William Morrow Paperbacks, 2001.

Borysenko, Joan. *The Power of the Mind to Heal.* Hay House, 1995.

Breathnach, Sarah Ban. *Something More: Excavating Your Authentic Self.* Grand Central Publishing, 2000.

Chopra, Deepak. *Ageless Body Timeless Mind: The Quantum Alternative to Growing Old.* Three Rivers Press, 1994.

Chopra, Deepak. *The Path to Love: Spiritual Strategies for Healing.* Three Rivers Press, 1998.

Chopra, Deepak. *The Seven Spiritual Laws for Parents: Guiding Your Children to Success and Fulfillment.* Three Rivers Press, 2006.

Chopra, Deepak. *The Seven Spiritual Laws of Success: A Practical Guide to the Fulfillment of Your Dreams.* New World Library/Amber-Allen Publishing, 1994.

Dossey, Larry. *Healing Words: The Power of Prayer & the Practice of Medicine.* HarperOne, 1991.

Dyer, Wayne W. *Pulling Your Own Strings: Dynamic Techniques for Dealing with Other People and Living Your Life as You Choose.* William Morrow Paperbacks, 1991.

Dyer, Wayne W. *Real Magic: Creating Miracles in Everyday Life.* William Morrow Paperbacks, 2001.

Dyer, Wayne W. *The Sky's the Limit.* Simon & Schuster, 1980.

Dyer, Wayne W. *Wisdom of the Ages: 60 Days to Enlightenment.* William Morrow Paperbacks, 2002.

Dyer, Wayne W. *You'll See It When You Believe It: The Way to Your Personal Transformation.* William Morrow Paperbacks, 2001.

Dyer, Wayne. W. *Your Erroneous Zones: Step-by-Step Advice for Escaping the Trap of Negative Thinking and Taking Control of Your Life.* William Morrow Paperbacks, 1991.

Eos, Nancy, M.D. *Reiki & Medicine.* Nancy Eos, 1995.

Estes, Clarissa Pinkola. *Women Who Run with the Wolves.* Ballantine Book, 1996.

Ford, Debbie. *The Dark Side of the Light Chasers.* Riverhead Trade, 2010.

Gawain, Shakti. *Creative Visualization: Use the Power of Your Imagination to Create What You Want in Your Life.* New World Library, Nataraj, 2002.

Gawain, Shakti and King, Laurel. *Living in the Light: Follow Your Inner Guidance to Create a New Life and a New World.* New World Library, 2011.

Gawain, Shakti. *Return to the Garden.* Nataraj Publishing, 1992.

Gerber, Richard. *Vibrational Medicine for the 21st Century: A Complete Guide to Energy Healing and Spiritual Transformation.* William Morrow, 2000.

Gibran, Khalil. *The Prophet.* Martino Fine Books, 2011.

Girsone, Joeseph. F. *Joshua: A Parable for Today.* Simon & Schuster/ Scribner, 1995.

Girsone, Joeseph. F. *Kara, The Lonely Falcon.* Scribner Paperback Fiction, 1997.

Grasberg, Lynn. *Bounce Back! The New Play Ethic at Work.* Morningstar Communications LLC, 2002.

Griscom, Chris. *Time is an Illusion.* Fireside; First Edition edition, 1988

Haye, Louise. *You Can Heal Your Life.* Hay House, 2009.

Holmes, Ernest. *Science of Mind.* SoHo Books, 2011.

Huddleston, Peggy. *Prepare for Surgery, Heal Faster: A Guide of Mind-Body Techniques.* Angel River Press, 1996.

Katie, Byron & Mitchell, Stephen. *Loving What Is: Four Questions That Can Change Your Life*. Three Rivers Press, 2003.

Keyes, Ken Jr. *Handbook to Higher Consciousness*. Living Love Center, 1976.

Lad, Vasant. *Ayurveda: The Science of Self Healing - A Practical Guide*. Lotus Press, 1993.

Lewis, Steven & Slawson, Evan. *Sanctuary*. Hay House, 2002.

Lama XIV, Dalai, Benson Ann, and Ouaki, Fabien. *Imagine All the People: A Conversation with the Dalai Lama on Money, Politics, and Life as It Could Be*. Wisdom Publications, 1999.

Matlin, Leni. *Ripples In A Pond*. Morningstar Communications LLC, 2002.

Mendelsohm, Robert S. M.D. *Confessions of a Medical Heretic*. Contemporary Books, 1979.

Myss, Carolyn. *Anatomy of the Spirit: The Seven Stages of Power & Healing*. Three Rivers Press, 1997.

Oz, Mehmet M.D. *Healing from the Heart: A Leading Heart Surgeon Explores the Power of Complementary Medicine*. Dutton Adult, 1998.

Piper, Mary PhD & Ross, Ruth. *Reviving Ophelia : Saving the Selves of Adolescent Girls*. Riverhead Trade, 2005.

Redfield, James. *The Celestine Prophecy*. Warner Books, Inc., 1997.

Redfield, James. *The Tenth Insight: Holding the Vision*. Grand Central Publishing, 1998.

Redfield, Salle Merrill. *The Joy of Meditating: A Beginner's Guide to the Art of Meditation*. Grand Central Publishing, 1995.

Roberts, Jane & Butts, Robert. F. *The Nature of Personal Reality: Specific, Practical Techniques for Solving Everyday Problems and Enriching the Life You Know*. Amber-Allen Publ., New World Library, 1994.

Roberts, Jane, Seth & Butts, Robert. F. *The Unknown Reality*. Amber-Allen Publishing, 1996.

Rosen, Peter. *The Luminous Life - How to Shine Like the Sun!* Roaring Lion, 1994.

Sher, Barbara. *I Could Do Anything If I Only Knew What It Was: How to Discover What You Really Want and How to Get It*. Dell, 1995.

Shubentsov, Yefim & Gordon, Barbara. *Cure Your Cravings: Learn to Use This Revolutionary System to Conquer Compulsions*. Perigee Trade, 1999.

Simpkins, C. Alexander PhD & Simpkins, Annellen. M. *Principles of Meditation.* Tuttle Publishing, 1996.

Svoboda, Robert E. *The Hidden Secret of Ayurveda.* Ayurvedic Press, 1996.

Walsh, Neale Donald. *Conversations With God: An Uncommon Dialogue (Book 1).* G. P. Putnam's Sons, 1996.

Walsh, Neale Donald. *Conversations With God: An Uncommon Dialogue (Book 2).* Hampton Roads Publishing Company, 1997.

Walsh, Neale Donald. *Conversations With God: An Uncommon Dialogue (Book 3).* Hampton Roads Publishing Company, 1998.

Walsh, Neale Donald. *Friendship with God: an uncommon dialogue.* Putnam Adult, 1999.

Warter, Carlos. *Recovery of the Sacred.* Hci, 1995.

Weil, Andrew. *Eight Weeks to Optimum Health, Revised Edition: A Proven Program for Taking Full Advantage of Your Body's Natural Healing Power.* Knopf, 2006.

Weil, Andrew. *Spontaneous Healing : How to Discover and Embrace Your Body's Natural Ability to Maintain and Heal Itself.* Ballantine Books, 2000

Wilde, Stewart. *Infinite Self: 33 Steps to Reclaiming Your Inner Power.* Hay House, 1996.

Wilde, Stewart. *Silent Power.* Hay House, 1998.

Wolf, Fred Allan. *Taking the Quantum Leap: The New Physics for Nonscientists.* Harper Perennial, 1989.

Yubat-Zinn, Jon. *Wherever You Go, There You Are (ROUGH CUT).* Hyperion, 2005.

Yubat-Zinn, Jon. *Full Catastrophe Living: Using the Wisdom of Your Body and Mind to Face Stress, Pain, and Illness.* Delta, 1990.

Zukav, Gary. *Dancing Wu Li Masters: An Overview of the New Physics.* HarperOne, 2001.

Unknown Author. *A Course in Miracles.*

Unknown Author. *Creating Miracles.*

Audio Cassettes

Abraham, Jay. *Your Secret Wealth.*

Altea, Rosemary. *Give the Gift of Healing.*

Borysenko, Joan PhD. *Meditation for Self Healing & Inner Power.*

Chopra, Deepak. *Ageless Body, Timeless Mind.*

Chopra, Deepak. *Magical Mind, Magical Body.*

Chopra, Deepak. *Sychro Destiny.*

Dyer, Wayne. *101 Ways to Transform Your Life.*

Dyer, Wayne. *Creating Your World the Way You Really Want It to Be.*

Dyer, Wayne. *Through the Wisdom of the Ages.*

Myss, Carolyn. *Spiritual Madness.*

Myss, Carolyn. *Why People Don't Heal and How They Can.*

Seigel, Bernie. *Healing From the Inside Out.*

Seigel, Bernie. *Humor & Healing.*

Sutphen, Dick. *Mind Travel.*

Wilde, Stuart. *Infinite Self.*

Williamson, Marianne. *Healing.*

About the Author

Dr. Edith del Mar Behr, Delmi to her friends is a surgeon who has mastered the art of mindful living and spiritual peace while thriving in the high-pressure world of surgery. She has a special interest in alternative medicine and a drive to share her story of finding calm in a world filled with stress.

In addition to her training as a physician and her experience treating patients as a whole, she has undertaken a comprehensive study of stress reduction and life enhancement methods, techniques and lifestyles. Dr. Behr has produced numerous articles on stress reduction and life enhancement as well as meditation and visualization recordings.

Dr. Behr gives seminars, clinics and is available for private sessions. She teaches practical methods of stress reduction to a broad range of personalities. She incorporates a number of methods that are simple to apply, making it possible for anyone, regardless of personal interest, religious or cultural affiliation, to benefit from attending.

Dr. Behr lives and practices medicine in Pottstown, Pennsylvania. She has two sons, Max and Hunter and five step children Lindsay, Michael, Jessica, Joseph and Autumn. For more information on Dr. Behr, visit *www.delmimd.com*

Made in the USA
San Bernardino, CA
03 November 2017